MARSHALL MAY

Utopia 2.0

First published by Creationatorium LLC 2023

First edition

ISBN: 979-8-9881296-1-5

This book was professionally typeset on Reedsy.
Find out more at reedsy.com

These were originally for my sons,
may they help you in life when I can't be there to guide the way

To Taj, for all the days we made each other think

To Ken, for making me realize these could be a book

To Sarah, for helping me in more ways than I could ever write
none of this would be possible without you
I love you

Contents

IV   Social Issues

V   Abuse of Power

Preface

My initial reason for writing this book and its thesis was in response to a growing movement in the world to remove freedom and personal responsibility from the ethos of our time. I've viewed the spreading of personal freedoms across the world as one of the most consequential developments in recorded history. As such, the removal of freedom seems to be a harbinger of death and decline in society. This realization, along with the births of my sons, has led me down a road of contemplation and discovery. It took me months of thought and personal deliberation to finalize my views on our society. In the end, I have this book. It was written to explain, to anyone who wishes to read, what I believe is a better way for society to be structured. This society can be structured so as to enhance the overall freedoms that we enjoy. In changing our society in these ways, I would hope to create what some would call a utopia of freedom. Due to my utter disdain for the governmental and societal structures laid out in the book "Utopia" by Thomas More, I have decided to take back the word utopia so as to return it to what it should have been: a place that can't exist, because it is different for everyone.

The first chapters in this book are meant to cover no single topic or specific harm to society. They assemble a framework that I believe would help society to move forward together even when people have disparate ideas of which political philosophy to follow.

Later chapters then lead into certain recommended changes on policy and law that should be taken in the hopes of altering our society towards a more peaceful and understanding civilization. Some of these changes are more philosophical than concrete, but they are important for how society sees itself.

Many problems that people have on a day-to-day basis can be distilled down to money problems. Whether it's not having enough for an emergency, not being able to save for the future, or simply not understanding the basics of money and the economy. I have put together my thoughts on what money is and what kind of limits the government should have in dictating how and when money is spent.

The majority of chapters within this book are dedicated to what I would call "hard" topics. What is a good monetary system? When should a nation go to war? How should a law be passed? Some of these chapters are about "soft" topics, as issues of conscience and morality. They weigh the morality of the individual versus the whole society, such as weighing the value of a child's life against that of a parent. These issues are not less important than a "hard" issue; they are more flexible in the answers that people prefer.

Lastly, I write about the failings of government and the actions that government has taken against the citizenry. I write about changes that would help make citizens trust in their government again, although many people have lost faith.

Thank you for your time. And thank you for giving my ideas a chance.

I

Generality of Laws

These chapters establish a framework for how to create, understand, and critique laws. This starts with a philosophical outlook on what type of ethical framework a person should hold and how to use that framework to craft laws. Next, I distinguish types of laws that I find to be inherently problematic, and describe how to create laws in a responsible manner. This will continue in a similar vein of logic, but will talk about the rules and regulations surrounding the passage of laws that I believe

1.1 Hierarchy of Ethics

As I have read through the political philosophies of the past, I realized that all of the conflicting theories for how to run a society seemed to be at odds. Some philosophers would extol the virtues of creating a society without greed while others would champion the maximization of greed. Issues always seem to arise when the ideals of a society are followed so closely that people from opposing worldviews are able to take advantage of loopholes within that philosophy itself. So, I have worked to create a framework for using multiple philosophies and ethical systems to create a nation's laws. This could potentially lead to fractalization of the political process. However, my framework would allow for changes to political platforms over the years, as the ethical hierarchy of party members change over time.

Pure Beliefs

A "Pure" belief is a system of thought or ethics that has been distilled down to its bedrock principles. Most ethical systems of thought have some bedrock principle that the entire system is built upon. For example, the belief of extreme non-violence or pacifism is the idea that all violence is unneeded and that any situation should be able to be solved without the use of violence. Belief in equity in the colloquial definition has come to mean something close to "equality of outcome". Utilitarians on the other hand believe in "the greatest good for the greatest number in the long run." There are times when you must choose between two actions, both are negative, but it is better to choose the lesser of two evils.

A society or nation that is built upon pacifism will operate differently than our nation. Laws that are written about murder and intentional harm to another person will be used infrequently and will potentially stop being prosecuted at all. Drunken brawls would start out as oddities that hardly ever occur, but the public pressure would eventually lead to them being all but eliminated. Similar issues such as domestic violence and road rage would eventually disappear. As that hypothetical develops, new laws would be made to focus more upon unintentional harm and any punishments that are required for the different circumstances that lead to someone being injured.

Formation of a society based on equity is easier to measure than to see. Across society, all jobs will be filled by an equal cross section of society. This will mean that all job types will have as close to 50% representation of male to female as possible. This would also be noticeable across nationalities, gender identity, language, economic background, education level, and much more. Such a nation might start out with incentive structures for diversity within jobs. The cultural ethos might start down a road praising diversity of background over everything else; this is already prevalent in higher level charity boards, but the ethos would eventually spread to all jobs. Eventually, hiring procedures might weigh an applicant's background so as to bring a better diversity of opinion to the company's internal decision making. This could lead to larger cultural homogenization, as more people are introduced to a larger set of cultural events and practices. Certain cultural events would become smaller and forgotten as others would be embraced and expanded even though the culture that originally celebrated such events has not grown in size. This will also lead to less misunderstanding between different outgroups as large miscommunications can be handled and diffused on a personal one-to-one level.

Basing a nation upon the idea of maximizing the public good is laudable. Laws would be put in place to make sure that those who suffer from extreme hardships would be helped. Regular audits of government departments would be mandated so as to quantify the amount of good each department has done for their intended recipients. And such audits would most likely be geared towards making sure those that receive benefits would not require benefits in the future. This would extend into the ethos of the population, citizens would make certain decisions based on maximizing fun over time without causing themselves issues in the future due to lack of funds. This would probably lead to moderation in spending with a larger interest in saving money for the future. I suspect that there would be a lower rate of businesses being started, but that there would also be a lower rate of failed businesses.

Taken To The Extreme

Each of the pure beliefs above can be used to create a lasting system of governance that will help their citizenry. However, there are times that a seemingly altruistic or benevolent system can be taken to a negative extreme.

A society based on non-violence will eventually find themselves in a position that any type of physical violence would be viewed as detestable and possibly even cause panic and distress for those that view the violence. There are cases of individuals now having PTSD from being present during a violent or traumatic event. In a society based upon pacifism for many generations, the idea of slapping someone would be unthinkable, let alone the thought of actually trying to kill someone. But if one person in the society decides that violence is acceptable, then they would be able to threaten, attack, or kill without the rest of the society knowing how to stop such a person. Police officers would be useless in this scenario, since they wouldn't have needed to deal with a violent individual during their career and they wouldn't have needed to be trained otherwise. The inability to cause violence makes such a society susceptible to any violent whims an individual might have; unless a new person "learns" how to use violence to remove the first person causing violence. However, that would mean that the society itself had changed from its pure state, and into one that would allow the use of violence in limited circumstances.

As the ideals of equity are spread, there comes an issue of leaving merit out of any decision making. A business wouldn't want to single out any one person or group that comes up with the best ideas; instead, managers would be instructed to equally promote and try the ideas of those that haven't had their ideas tried recently. This would also mean that any position that opens up higher on the corporate ladder would need to be filled with someone with either a similar background or of a more diverse background that is lacking from that section of the company. Then their position would need to be filled by someone similar to them, and on and on until a new hire is made at the bottom most rung of the ladder. Corporations would stop being run by those that have gone to a business school or have started their own business. Corporations would be run by groups of token individuals that are considered the "most diverse" among their peers. The more diverse you are, the faster you would go up the corporate ladder. This would incentivise an individual to "other" themselves, to find things about themselves that are different from the rest of society and to make sure everyone knows that it is part of their identity.

Utilitarianism is a philosophy that I find interesting from an intellectual perspective; the idea that sometimes a person must choose an action that does harm but that it is better overall than all other alternatives makes sense to me. The concern I have is that there will always be a subjective element to such actions that make utilitarianism highly malleable to the whims of those in charge. Who decides what is "the greatest good" and who decides what percentage of the population is acceptable to change? The answer again, in the real world rather than the ideal Utilitarian world, is whomever has the power at the moment. What happens when scientists discover a way to give a permanent hit of dopamine that will never stop being effective à la Huxley's a brave new world? Wouldn't it be better to mandate that everyone be forced to use the new drug? Wouldn't it be a better world if no one was allowed to leave a pod where all of your food is provided for you? No one would go hungry, and no one would die from accidents. What if a worldwide famine hit; should we kill 25% of the population of earth who are determined to be the saddest? We needed to kill someone due to the food shortage and the majority of people would statistically be happier because all of the remaining people would have a happier outlook on life. After that "worked" so well, we could just kill anyone that gets depressed, so that there are no more unhappy people in the world. What types of people would be able to get sad with infinite dopamine, enough food, and shelter? Wouldn't that be "the greatest good for the greatest number in the long run"?

Part of the issue with these examples is that the extreme purity of the idea causes unintended consequences. In fact, the purer an idea becomes, the more likely there is someone able to disrupt that system with an opposing belief system. Most people are fine with non-violence, but most people also realize that sometimes violence is required for the system to continue. And the more pure the society becomes about non-violence, the more likely there will be someone that decides to throw off the ideals of the society and rebel against it.

Choose Your System

Any personal system of beliefs should be built on a bedrock of pure belief(s). If you want a country to protect its citizens from hostile invaders, then the pure belief of protection or military strength would be good contenders. If instead you want a government to regulate the sale of goods then the pure belief of honesty and trust could be taken as ideals. In fact, you should try to find multiple pure beliefs that will make up your bedrock ethics. Finding beliefs that compliment each other is better than adopting opposing beliefs that might cause difficulty when creating rules, unless clear boundaries for the beliefs are created beforehand. As an example, freedom of religion and free markets don't have opposing views that require boundaries beforehand, but such boundaries might be required later. In the case of freedom of speech and freedom from insults, these two beliefs come into direct opposition. Clear boundaries with limits on each belief will mitigate but not prevent issues in the future. When deciding on boundaries, if there is a clear divide on which belief has the higher preference in the system, then the preferred belief should stay as a bedrock principle and the other one should be pushed to a lower level of the hierarchy.

Now that your bedrock principles have been chosen, picking your secondary principles comes into play. Your secondary layer should be close ethically to your bedrock beliefs with some areas where you have disagreements. A tertiary belief will be further away than secondary, and on and on until you have listed all ethical systems into your hierarchy. Some layers will have more systems than others and no set formula has yet been proven to work. By the end of creating your own hierarchy there will be a lot of polar opposite viewpoints from many different systems within the rankings. In fact, I recommend not boxing yourself into listing political parties. Instead think of the principles that those political parties represent and then rank them on your hierarchy. You will see how there will be some political party principles that rise higher than their other beliefs due to their ability to be viewed on their own instead of dealing with the political party as a whole. Your hierarchy should shift and change over time as you find out new things and learn about issues in the world. As a young man I remember believing highly in "Safety" and "Military Power", but over the years "Non-Interventionism" has grown in prominence. Revisiting your hierarchy and adjusting your beliefs can be important.

Creating Rules and Laws

Besides bedrock principles, a nation is established with its own hierarchy based on the constitution and laws that it passes. Each time a new law is adopted, the hierarchy of principles is shifted to fit the nation's laws. This can mean that citizens that grew up under a specific way of living can slowly find that their nation has changed into something unrecognizable.

So let's create an example of a law for a hypothetical nation. For a nation to create a law it should start from its bedrock principles. We will use the bedrocks of freedom of belief, freedom of association, and personal responsibility. These beliefs are shared with a great many different groups and many people agree with them in principle. So the initial law that follows these principles would most likely be one curtailing the government and its citizens from interfering with someone's right to meet with others and discuss any topic they freely choose to discuss. This would need to include topics that would be considered inappropriate or in bad taste such as advocating for pornography in TV commercials. Remember, freedom is only freedom if it applies to the things you don't like just as equally to those you do. Part of the law should show that the government is unable to retaliate against those that discuss an inappropriate topic in public. Those not in government remain free to disassociate from those discussing an inappropriate topic. The second clause is in place to highlight personal responsibility: everyone is responsible for understanding what is socially acceptable to discuss or to halt discussion when it is made clear that an issue has arisen. If the person refuses to stop, then the social pressure of people refusing to associate with them might change their mind.

Now it is time to search for loopholes or issues with current law. Property will be my illustration. One issue is if your speech and discussion is happening on property that isn't your own. Language in the law should explain that the owner or their representative should be able to make you leave their property. This rule would fall under freedom of association, as the owner is free to not associate with you for any reason. This might be made tricky when the property is open to the public, like a store or park. Laws may allow for certain limits of speech such as its volume, so as to make sure others can use the facilities as well. While this is a restriction or limit placed on the bedrock beliefs, the addition of such rules allow for the usage of the public space and accommodations in a way that doesn't stop the casual usage of other people. This restriction, because it does not fit into the bedrock belief, means that it should be as narrowly tailored as possible to fix the issue at hand. As such, more leeway might be given to the store owner to limit what kind of people can use their establishment. Such limitations might include a loitering policy or the ability to restrict "rowdy" behavior. Limitations would allow for the store to not be required to host individuals for an excessive amount of time more than the average customer would spend in the store, or in a sense, they aren't required to associate with the individuals more than they would normally be required to with any other member of the public.

As the law is expanded and loopholes are patched, the rules that go against the bedrock principles should accentuate them. As an example, the limit on public shops or stores from kicking out customers that discuss inappropriate topics restricts the police and other government agents from asking stores to preemptively ban individuals from stores or from following individuals to harass them at stores to ask them to leave. This makes sure that individuals are allowed to speak their thoughts and work through issues that trouble them without the fear of backlash from society. That freedom of speech permits discussion of controversial issues that could be detrimental to society as a whole. What if the issue being discussed is a public official that raped multiple people? The inappropriate topic would potentially allow the police to harass anyone who wanted to inform the public about the issue.

An Analogy

For this example, please imagine an open location with an object sitting in the middle of the open space. This object will symbolize all of the "good" things that your nation has to offer to its citizens or to the world at large. In essence, that good is the reason why anyone would like to live in your nation. If this object is left unguarded, then anyone would be able to change or damage the object as they see fit. So your nation makes laws, in this analogy, to be like bricks that are placed together to build a wall. As the wall is built, you have to build it from the perspective of the pure belief that your nation is constructed upon.

Once the wall is built, anyone with the same pure belief structure of the nation would be kept from doing harm to the nation's object. But, if you were to alter the perspective that you're viewing the wall by, then you would see holes that have been left in your previously solid wall. These holes are available to anyone with the belief system you are currently looking from. So, you can use bricks that work in this perspective to plug up the holes in the wall. Now you can shift to the perspective of a third belief system, where the amount of holes in the wall should be less than the amount of holes from the preceding system. This will be due to not only the original system's bricks but also the second system's bricks which are also protecting the object in the center. This hypothetical nation should begin by patching holes from the belief systems that resonate with the nation's pure beliefs first, and then gradually move down the hierarchy of ethics until the possible holes are patched to prevent the ways people would be able to abuse the system and gain access to the object.

To expand upon this example I will show how using this framework would work in relation to a currently contentious topic within American politics, Transgender Rights. I will start from the wide latitude of freedom that America fosters within the nation. There is no evidence of anything inherently dangerous or harmful to someone that is transgender or to those around them, so it should be illegal for the government to forbid a person from freely identifying or presenting as a gender different from their original biological sex. This solves the issue from the perspective of a "live and let live" perspective, but not all Americans would think of this issue as solved. So let's view this issue from the perspective of discrimination. Adding sexual orientation to the list of protected characteristics would ensure that no one can refuse service from a public accommodation such as a restaurant, hotel, public transportation, or any store open to the public. Ensuring that anyone living a peaceful life can use such services available to the public contributes to the values that I believe America was founded upon.

A similar issue is employment discrimination, so making sure that an employer is unable to treat someone differently based on sexual orientation should also be important. Next we shift to the issue of medical availability. Some trans-activists have asked the government to guarantee a lower cost for their medical transition, surgeries, and aftercare. This seems to me to go too far. No citizen should be refused emergency care from an ER, but such treatments are not emergency medicine. Instead they are elective procedures that each person must decide if they are able to afford.

On the slightly different topic of mental fitness, I believe that America should make sure that its ideals of freedom are taken seriously and that any deprivation of rights is scrutinized as much as possible. As I have said earlier, there is no evidence that someone who is transgender is inherently dangerous or harmful to themselves or others. So any discussions about mental fitness based solely on sexual orientation should be completely disregarded.

Shifting to the ability to serve in the Military, I see no good reason to forbid transgender soldiers as long as they can pass any of the standard tests that a recruit is required to pass for the position they wish to fill. My only issue depends on the personal medical requirements for the individual soldier, especially if that soldier is meant to be sent to a war theater. Some transgender individuals require a constant supply of medication depending on where they are in their transition, and sometimes they require permanent use of drugs after the transition as well. Would such drugs be life threatening if they aren't taken? Would an issue of supply lines on the battlefield make such a soldier a liability? Could the soldier hold off on part of their transition until after they finish their service? I would be in favor of anyone that wishes to join the military and protect their nation to do so, but I also see the potential downside that a stable military must work around.

Overall, if the legal patches are done correctly, you should need fewer and fewer patches as you go down the hierarchy. However, there may be multiple layers of bricks covering the same areas. This is not a problem, since this can be seen as a feature that protects the nation from some of the worse problems that can happen.

I expect and encourage each change to a nation's laws to be vigorously debated and verbally contested. Each section of a law should be tailored to fit the required space and expected to change for the purposes of testing any future hypothetical "better way of doing things". These changes will eventually lead to an eventual "best practices" that most will take as a forgone conclusion. But even those changes will be susceptible to further change if there is a potentially better way of doing things that needs to be tested; even if that testing is in a limited program of a limited area by willing participants that wish for the change to occur.

A Nations Beliefs Over Time

The bedrock principles of a nation will alter over time. When they do change, that change will usually be slight, and align with the original bedrock beliefs. They might become broader changes to incorporate a larger set of issues, or they may distill down into more specific issues while other similar issues are left behind. Even a complete flip to an opposing view is possible, however unlikely, and that flip would usually only be due to large political or social pressure from within the nation. Part of the issue for dealing with such change is that smaller changes will be easier for the mind of the populace to accept as the new order. Larger changes require more evidence to the contrary and will be more likely to be dismissed outright as wrong.

I believe in the 20% rule that is needed to change someone's mind. When an individual is forming an opinion on a subject, they must first find data to support a conclusion. Whether this data is scholarly research articles, first hand accounts, or wild speculation doesn't matter. What matters is that the first conclusion must be backed by at least 51% of the evidence available, and that evidence could be as flimsy as "my father told me so". But after the initial conclusion has been made, the amount of evidence needed to believe the opposing side is no longer 51%. Instead you would need at least a 20% difference to be swayed to the opposing side. This is also not a guarantee that their mind will be changed at 20%. There will be more hard-headed individuals that require more proof for their mind to be changed. It can also be a bit of a losing battle when trying to find opposing evidence, because older information that you agree with if re-stated can be considered new information. The same study or personal anecdote can be seen as two data points helping the original opinion win out over any new beliefs systems.

Advocacy for your bedrock beliefs and showing how it has helped within existing laws is the best way to change opinions about your beliefs. That way, those that would usually oppose the inclusion of your bedrock principles will become agreeable to the usage of similar changes to other laws. Eventually, their minds may change so that your beliefs are an acceptable part of society. On the other hand, you should never expect to eliminate an opposing political bedrock principle in its entirety. Trying to stamp out an opposing side will just lead to a potential political resurgence or hidden political movements that allow for radicalization to occur due to the lack of opposing viewpoints.

As the bedrock principles of a country change over time, the laws of that country will change to meet the new beliefs. This can happen through active augmentation of the laws on the books, or through apathy of police action.

1.2 Specificity and Broadness

One of the largest issues that plagues the laws of this overly political world is how difficult it is for the average person to understand the twisting nuances within the laws. Some laws are made with small carve-outs for individual groups that change and alter over time, and others are made to deal with such a large amount of issues that any one thing can be lost in the whole and never fleshed out. Such laws create issues for those that must obey. I propose that all laws should keep specificity and broadness in mind. Specificity of topic and words would make laws that are more easily searchable and understood by the typical person. Broadness about the people that the law applies to prevents legislators from carving out special exemptions for their own benefit.

Specificity

The first thing to ask when making a law is "What will this law be about?". The law in question must have a defined purpose and limitations on where the law may apply is important. Laws that are too vague as to what subject they are about while being written are usually doomed to expansive rules and regulations that impact large sections of laws with varying levels of success. On the other hand, a law that is too specific is possible but less likely to occur, and when it does, they tend to be used infrequently. In reality, the question to be asked is "Can this be more specific?" and if it can, then it should be.

An issue that can occur with vague laws is the unintended usage of the law. Vagueness in the law can be used positively when trying to forestall technicalities; a law against murder doesn't have to list all of the ways someone can be murdered for it to be illegal. Instead, the law just has to give a generic statement of what constitutes a murder. On the other hand, a law can be vague enough to allow for unintended criminal charges to be made. Examples? Getting charged with hacking because the person logged into the company server to check their email using the password they were originally given. This was seen as a misinterpretation of the spirit of the law, even though they were following the letter of it. An explanation of the crime of hacking can be broad to make sure that any future crimes using different technologies wouldn't be legal just due to the technological difference. Finding a balance in the wording of the law is important for anyone writing laws for public use.

Using the correct meaning for words is another issue where specificity matters a great deal. The use of words that have colloquial definitions is important, because laws are meant for the general public. Similarly, words that have vastly different colloquial definitions from their legal definition shouldn't be used. To this point, a law should be encouraged to define as many words as possible to make sure the spirit of the law is understood after the fact. In fact, a version of a legal dictionary should be kept by any governing body, in which it lists all words that the governing body has defined in law. Multiple entries should be made for every way that the word is defined, even slight differences, and should be listed with the date it was passed into law and which law it was passed under. This makes it impossible to change the law by changing what certain words mean after the fact.

Lastly, a law is specific when it does not cover a broad range of topics or issues. Laws should be about one thing, and not split into other subjects. This could be as small and innocent as making a law against murder, where the first half of the legislation is entirely about the crime of murder and then a small section talks about the issues of burglary and then continues to talk about murder for the rest of the law. The only way that would be reasonable is if the law was referencing why something was not the crime the law was about and instead pointed towards the crime it would fall under. But even then, the law shouldn't be pointing towards the other crime. If they wanted to clarify the law on burglary then they should write a different law that regulates that clarification. It is fine to make legislation about multiple subjects that are closely related if the intent of the law is specifically about these subjects. The issue arises when smaller subjects are shoe-horned into legislation where they aren't needed or required.

Broadness

The main reason to be broad is to promote equality and parity of the law between individuals. Laws should be targeted at actions that hurt society, not targeted at individuals or groups that have drawn the ire of those that write the laws. As such, a law that doesn't regulate the actions of at least 80% of the population should be voided for being too narrow. That being said, even limiting the law to 90% of the population should be looked down upon. Whenever possible, making a law apply to 100% of the population is preferable and should be lauded.

Some will ask how a law that regulates gendered issues can apply to 100% of the population since it can by definition only pertain to around half of the population. I posit that the law in question is not broad enough – there is no issue that doesn't apply to both sexes in some way. Reciprocal rules between the sexes is important; in fact, I believe that there is no law required for society to function that only applies to one gender. Any law for one gender should be extended to the other gender with whatever changes are needed to make it reciprocal. One of the issues where this has been made clear to me is abortion. A woman that decides to get a legal abortion faces no reprisals, but there is no legal form of an abortion that a man can decide to take part in. This means that any man is put at the whims of the woman that holds all of the power after conception. If we decide to allow women to abort the child within a certain period after becoming pregnant, then allowing a man to have a financial abortion within a certain period after becoming aware of the pregnancy would be considered reciprocal. For context, the idea of a financial abortion is the idea that a man could opt out of fatherhood by signing away his rights to the child and in return would not be required to provide any legal or financial support to the child. This is similar to the issue of whether or not a woman wants to put her child up for adoption, she has no responsibilities legally or financially to the child once the adoption has gone through. The same thing should be available to any man that wants to put his child up for adoption. If the law isn't equal, then it needs to be either broadened to encompass a larger section of society or voided.

Issues can arise when a law technically applies to everyone but is tailored to only apply to a smaller group of individuals. Such an issue is not applicable to laws regulating the ethical treatment of medical patients. Anyone that is treating someone medically must follow the ethical standards of the law, and the law doesn't distinguish if you are treating them as a licensed physician or as a homeopathic technician. There is an issue when the law regulates water usage, but only by farmers. Why is it that a farmer that must use 20,000 gallons of water a day for the production has to be limited, but the water park 5 miles away could dump the same amount into its parking lot and no one could complain. In fact, this would probably create a perverse incentive for someone to create a black market for water; since they aren't pumping the water themselves, the act of using the water might not be illegal under the law in question. An easy solution would be to regulate the usage of all water: the limit might mainly affect farmers, but in the end everyone would be under the same limitations.

Any law that allows for special dispensation should be considered suspect.

Firstly, the issue of who would be allowed this special dispensation shows an inherent bias for or against those with a political bias. Imagine if only 20% of applications of special dispensation are granted, then it would be easy to use this power as a cudgel against an adversary or allow all applications for your friends and allies. This has been shown to be true in "may issue" gun license states where certain jurisdictions only allow the politically connected to obtain a permit while the average citizen will always be denied. Any discretion left to a political officer or bureaucrat would create the possible appearance of impropriety; and rightly so, all bureaucracy should be done in the light of day because any bureaucracy done in secret should be suspect at best. The other issue with special dispensation is the question of why it isn't affirmed in law. As an example, what if instead of allowing for a special permit to be received, the law stated that meeting certain requirements made it legal without a permit. This would require a law or executive to list all requirements, so that the inability to create a suitable list of requirements that doesn't require the use of a subjective test would be worrisome for the efficacy of the law. As I see it, feelings are fluid while the law must be steadfast. Skepticism should be shown towards any law that was written with the explicit intent of giving an executive power over deciding the legality of something. A lawmaker must be able to write down a list of requirements for something to be legal.

The last issue of broadness is dealing with immutable characteristics. Any law that divides people into groups based on immutable characteristics is abhorrent and should be stricken and remade. An immutable trait or characteristic is one that once determined can never be changed or altered at will; if a change is possible, then the requirement to change must be extensive or risky. Some traits are race, ethnicity, place or birth, family ties, culture, and nationality. Sexual orientation is also considered immutable because a person is unable to reasonably choose who they are attracted to. As such, making a law against being a lesbian would mean the law would only apply to the small percentage of women that happen to be lesbians, making the law in itself too narrow. What you can legislate would be a sexual act that anyone can do; oddly enough, that makes sodomy law technically acceptable since anyone is able potentially give blowjobs and receive anal sex. What this does not allow sexually is pedophilia; the issue at hand for pedophilia is consent, not attraction. Religion is another immutable trait due to the extensive process involved in the change. Being brought up in a religion as a child makes the process of change to no religion or a different religion more difficult. It should also be a protected act to change religions or to leave all religions behind. We can't make it artificially harder to change so that it becomes immutable.

1.3 The Passing of Laws

The laws of a country should be read and debated by any and all citizens that are so civically minded. Instead, I find that the laws being passed are written in such a way that no one but lawmakers would willingly read them in their entirety. And those laws are permanent fixtures that require enough political will power to overturn. These issues and some other smaller problems have made me realize that some changes to how laws are passed is sorely needed.

Topic Limit

An issue that permeates most laws is how broad laws are allowed to be. Each law should be limited to a single subject, and that subject should be explained at the outset of the bill writing. If a bill deviates from the specified topic, then that section of the bill should be thrown out; if the section can't be eliminated without creating issues elsewhere in the same bill, then the entire bill needs to be thrown out. Large omnibus bills that have broad reaching effects over entire swaths of the economy, public land, and/or criminal statutes are a burden on the average citizen trying to learn about what laws are being passed. This will also solve the issue of lawmakers making backroom deals for side projects that have nothing to do with the current legislation; such backroom deals should be eliminated all together, but there will always be ways for politically connected individuals to push passion projects through the legislature. But for now, we should be happy to make sure there are no more crime bills that have a three line addition for a park to be built in a specific district.

Standardization

At first glance, the issue of standardizing each law that is to be passed might seem a bit ridiculous. An issue arises not when a limit is put onto lawmakers, but for excessive wiggle room that is given and then taken advantage of in the attempt to get away with more than they normally would. As such, the government should create a custom or standard font that they are required to use when writing laws. The actual appearance of the font doesn't matter, but should be easily read by anyone that has been educated in a public school. Anyone should be allowed to use that font, and in fact the government should consider using the font on any official documents or forms produced by a government office. Next should be a standard layout for how a bill or law is to be structured, anything from whether a cover page is required and what the cover page is to include, all the way to the size of the typeface for the body of texts. Further requirements should cover the size should the borders around the page be, is the spacing set to single or double, how are heading and subheadings to be inserted into the legislation, what about sections and subsections of a law, and the formatting of footnotes, graphs, and charts. All of these things and more should be standardized so that every law written should be able to be read by any citizen.

Sunset Clauses

Laws should either be so popular that the mere fact that they exist should be expected or that any law that happens to pass by the skin of its teeth should be revisited from time to time. So sunset clauses should be considered mandatory on all laws and should have different lengths of time depending on the percentage of people that voted for the bill unless such overwhelming support for the bill or law is shown. As depicted in the table below.

Sunset in Years	Percentage of Votes
1 Year	51%
5 Years	55%
15 Years	60%
30 Years	65%
50 Years	70%
75 Years	75%
None	80% or above

Amendments to the constitution are not susceptible to sunset clauses due to the rigorous standard that has to be reached. And any law that is set to expire can have its sunset reset on an expedited time frame as long as some extra stipulations are met. 50% of the original sunset is needed to get passed, and this keeps legislators from passing a bill and then judging if the bill would have passed at a higher percentage and then asking for a larger sunset. Nothing from the original bill can be altered except for the length of sunset, to allow for the nation to make a law permanent when the time comes that an overwhelming section of the populace agrees with the bill. This also prevents a politician from secretly altering the bill from its original intent without starting from scratch. This also means that a bill shouldn't be able to pass if it changes something that once changed can't be undone at a later date unless such a groundswell of the general population is backing the bill so that it becomes permanent.

Bill Length

Laws should be as short as possible, and any law that is excessively long should be suspect and should have a tougher time passing. If a bill is so long that it can't get enough votes to pass, that means that the law should be removed from consideration. Hopefully this will encourage smaller laws that will work together to change things over time, as well as the ability to change small issues within a bill without having to fight over large contentious issues. The lengths of a bill vs required percentage of votes are depicted in the table below.

Length of Bill	Percentage of Votes
15 Pages	51%
20 Pages	60%
25 Pages	70%
30 Pages	80%
35 Pages	90%
40 Pages	100%

To be honest, one of the driving factors for this push to decrease the amount of pages used in the writing of a bill is to allow for the average citizen to engage in civics more easily. I want a school teacher to be able to assign their 8th grade class a bill that is currently before Congress, to be read and then debated in class in a week's time. I want citizens to feel like the bills being passed are able to be read easily and so don't contain large amounts of useless information that bloat the bill to the point of uselessness or even hide expenditures that the average person wouldn't approve.

When They Are Determined

Both the length of and the sunset associated with a bill should be determined before any debate or vote on the bill in question. This would prevent brinkmanship over passing a law and then rewriting or fitting the sunset to fit the allowed limits. In practice, there is no requirement for a bill to be

25 pages long and also have a sunset of 50 years. Passing the law might be easier if those voting on it knew that it would only be applicable for 5 years. Issues can be forced upon the bill during the debating of the bill. An ability to add more pages to the document needs to be limited to the point that if a bill comes to the floor with a limit of 25 pages, then any additions can't push the bill into a higher page limit. Similarly, the ability to change the sunset amount once the bill is put forward is stopped until the bill passes and is then brought back up to reset the sunset. I would suggest also limiting the amount of times someone can re-introduce legislation for consideration so as to make it impossible to set an artificially high sunset and then once it fails bringing the sunset down to the point where it would pass. But as it is, that level of minutiae of rules should be up to those in Congress to set.

Counting Of Votes

For a bill to be passed into a law, it must first be discussed and debated in an open session of Congress. Once the debate has been concluded, a vote on the bill must be done. All votes must be counted and tallied with the distinction of who voted "for", "against", "abstained", or was "not present". Vote tallies are to be made public at all times so that any citizen can know the voting record of their or any other congressman or woman. Asking for the yays and nays, and then not actually counting those who voted is not allowed, because every law should be given the same gravity as all other laws because they affect all citizens the same. If for any reason the counting of votes is interrupted, then the partial tally is to be recorded, the remaining present are to be labeled as "abstained", and any not present are to be labeled as "not present". Anyone that was labeled as "abstained" will be allowed to change their vote to either "for" or "against" within a reasonable amount of time. Once the counting is interrupted, the same bill without any changes will be eligible to be voted on again once the issue that halted voting has been resolved. If for some reason, another interruption takes place, the votes that have been counted can be locked in place and then the remaining votes can be taken without needing to redo the initial votes. This can continue until all members have a recorded vote and the bill either passes or fails.

Only votes that reach a minimum of 60% of possible seats in attendance for the vote will count. If a bill is not able to reach such a low bar, then the bill must not be of sufficient enough interest at that time for it to pass. This also applies to any bill that is voted on during an emergency session; if the emergency session is unable to put forth 60% of all total seats during an emergency then the bill must not be seen as important enough. If there are not enough active members to reach the targeted goal of 60%, that would mean that a true emergency has happened and I will point you to the upcoming chapter called "Emergency Powers". However, if an emergency session is able to be called and is able to produce more that 60% of total seats for a vote, then that law will automatically be subject to the lowest page length and sunset. This is a penalty for not bringing such legislation up during a standard session, and will hopefully encourage a more formal bill to be brought up during the next standard session so as to replace the emergency bill.

For clarification purposes, all percentages of votes discussed are calculated based on total possible seats, not on active members or members in attendance at that time. So if the Senate has 100 seats, then the percentage will always refer to how many people voted in the affirmative out of 100; not out of the 98 filled seats because 2 died in car accidents, or the 83 that are in attendance for the vote. This might seem obvious, but you would be surprised as to the ridiculous amount of specificity someone needs to have when dealing with people that twist the meaning of words for a living.

Exception To The Rules

The only bill that can supersede the requirements of bill length will be one entirely focused on budget. This does mean that if any portion of the bill adds to or alters the laws of the country, then it must follow the rules of length and sunset. Since a budget bill is only technically applicable for 1 year anyways, the sunset would be set to 1 year and can't be altered. If a new budget isn't passed by the following Congress then they will have given a tacit consent that the previous year's budget is acceptable with the removal of all non-budgetary sections in the bills. A true budgetary bill will only approve the usage of money for predetermined bills that have been voted on. I am not making it a hard and fast rule that no budget bill can be passed with a rule change in it, but I am recommending that the bill should be easily read through to determine the changes to any laws. Also, this would identify any special circumstance that was needed to pass a portion of the budget in the first place.

1.4 Issues In A Law

The writing of laws means that sometimes the writers will misunderstand the consequences of the laws they wish to enact. New issues will be created solely due to a law that was meant as a solution to the first problem. Sometimes the writer of the law has a fundamental lack of knowledge about the issues at hand and the proposed law would do nothing to help. At other times they won't take into account a facet of human nature that either caused the problem in the first place or how people would react to the new regulation. The next logical question when such an issue is found should be how to solve such an issue in the law.

Not All Issues Can Be Solved

As the name of this section states, not all issues can be solved. Some of this is from the fact that all issues and the solutions to them have a subjective value or harm based on the person being asked. Sometimes the harm that an issue is causing will be obvious, but there will be many times that the harm is either not clear or it will take time for the issue to show itself. Realizing this, you must be prepared to deal with others that might not want to change the law because they either don't see the issue or actually wanted the issue to occur.

Until a utopia is reached, and most likely even after that, all societies will generate issues due to the way that we are all human. Not all of those issues should be solved, because there are times individuals need adversity to grow. Societal pressure can be a safe and easy way to help mold a person into a better version of themself. Issues could also be derived from biological or sociological imperatives that drive us as humans. And trying to solve such imperatives can be detrimental to society as a whole, especially when trying to force such a change through the use of laws.

Some solutions will be partial fixes for the issue at hand, but the new pain will be a better alternative. Such outcomes are difficult to determine with a high accuracy due to individual preferences. Finding whether or not society is hurt by the consequences of a law can be so subjective depending on the morality of those being asked. But, asking how is society hurt by this law and if the law leaves society better off in aggregate is important. This can also lead to the issue of someone writing the law with what you view as an issue baked into the law as a feature. This is why it is important to make laws easier to read, the ability for more people to parse out potential issues in a law and then debate the possible issues that will arise from their implementation will make society more cohesive and understanding.

Mitigating the harmful effects of a law after they become an issue might have to be enough. This is usually more acceptable when the issue a law is made to stop is such a detriment to society that any delay could cause irreparable harm. Running the chance that an issue will eventually crop up is worthwhile. Being able to give society more time to solve the initial issue can be the main goal, but eventually society might have to solve the new issue that has arisen separately. Solving one problem that will lead into a second issue, and onto a third and fourth, is no way to run a society. How many times are you willing to play "whack-a-mole" with an entire nation's laws before you cut your losses and deal with the issues in a new and more rational way?

Unintended Consequence

Unintended consequences are when a law creates a scenario that the public didn't expect the law to create. This could be a positive, negative or neutral issue. Such a consequence would include an issue that was created by California's banning of plastic bags. It was never taken into account that the homeless population used the plentiful plastic bags they could get for free to clean up after themselves. So, when the law banning the bags went into effect, the cleanliness of areas with large homeless populations fell drastically. Any unintended consequence is the product of the writer of the law not understanding how people or society at large would react to the law in question. Anyone writing laws should try to eliminate such consequences before passing the bill into law.

Perverse Incentive

A perverse incentive is when a law creates a scenario in which someone receives a benefit for doing something bad. This can never be considered a "good thing", in fact, the issue the law creates is usually considered universally bad. As an example, welfare was meant to help families that fell onto bad times. But, single mothers were deemed to need more help than families with both parents; so they made the payments to single mothers higher. This has been linked to a dramatic rise in the rate of single motherhood. Why this is happening is contested, but no one is contesting the fact that it is a problem that the law most likely caused. Perverse incentives require the repeal or reconfiguring of the law in question and should be mitigated every time one is found. The large-scale societal damage that can be done from leaving a perverse incentive is difficult to understate. Many researchers link the single mother rate to many other issues that affect society as a whole and can even have generational issues when children that grow up with perverse incentives taught to them as if it was a normal part of society.

What "Level" Of Fix Is Required

Fixing issues in a law comes down to four methods. Each of these methods are applicable, but are not always able to solve all of the issues in a law. Finding out which solution will work for which problem is important.

Removal Of The Program

Sometimes the most extreme solution is the only solution to the issue, completely removing the law or program in question. Usually this type of solution is required when the original law was based upon a flawed premise and it was trying to solve an issue that either doesn't exist or has no relation to what is in the law. As an example, the government wanted to reduce racist practices in the loan process. So, they decided to loosen restrictions for banks to lend money safely and even incentivised giving loans to minority communities even if they didn't qualify for the loans in the first place. This caused loan defaults and foreclosures to rise exponentially in minority communities; a lot of the generational wealth that was built up by those communities were wiped out due to the housing crash. The idea of eliminating racist lending practices from the lending process is laudable, but the way the law went about doing it is wrong at its core. So the only way to move forward and remove the perverse incentive is to stop the program in its entirety and to start over from step one.

Shifting The Goal

Altering what the program is trying to fix, to a more attainable goal is another method. Instead of removal of the program all together, making such large changes to the program to the point where it will solve the issue through an entirely different method is easier in the sense that the money and resources are already in place to make a change; but more difficult because this requires reworking the existing law to make a brand new program. As an example, there are community programs to help those that don't have enough money for food. Eliminating child hunger through food banks is useful and effective, but there are some communities that have a large stigma attached to the use of such programs. Instead, there is an option to allow for free school lunches and breakfasts; this would create a stigma-free environment for children to receive food from the government and to not worry about where their next meal will come from. A side benefit of this is a potential reduction in the stigma associated with using government assistance in the area when the children that have fond memories of receiving free food when they were hungry grow into adults. The change was to shift from a goal of feeding hungry families, to specifically feeding hungry children.

Change The Solution

The next option is to change how the program solves the problem, while this is sometimes difficult to differentiate from "shifting the goal" the difference is important. Where the previous method changed the goal of the program, changing the method the program uses to reach the same goal shows that the goal is the important part. Homelessness can be a problem for very large cities, and for smaller towns as well that don't have enough resources to start up a dedicated homelessness solution. Some cities find that homeless people refuse to use shelters even if they are provided by the city for various reasons. Changing the solution to getting someone a safe job with a company that understands the issues of being homeless and possibly even giving them monetary compensation for giving them the chance could change enough about the homeless person's life to get them off the street. This could be helped along by another part of the program where a cheaper rental rate could be given to stay at a long term hotel as long as they continue to work. These two methods of solving the problem of homelessness if done together would help those that wish to raise themselves out of the situation they are in; and that is all that a government can do. You can lead a horse to water, but you can't make it drink.

Alter Data Points

This last way of changing a program is probably the easiest to accomplish once the change has been decided upon, but just as difficult as the others. Making a change of individual data point(s) within the existing program is useful when most of the plan has worked or the psychology behind the program has worked, but that there are issues with some inner workings of the plan are causing problems. This could be as small as altering an amount of money that is given to each participant of the program, or even altering the criteria for who is eligible to join the program as a participant. Such small changes can sometimes have vast and wide reaching effects.

Lets use an example of a welfare program that incentivises single motherhood by offering single women with children more money than those that are part of a joint household. If we alter the amount to be given to single mothers to be equal to or less than if the father is still in the house, then the incentive to remove the father from the house is gone. This would also remove the negative effects of less money for stable families and would potentially help those families stay together. Similarly, the option of increasing benefits for a stable family would actually incentivise families to stay together and find solutions to their issues. An issue could arise where the family that is better off separated would try to make things work so that they don't lose out on benefits, causing a new potential unintended consequence of prolonged domestic abuse in certain families.

II

Not Laws, But A Nation

In this section, I will discuss land rights and who has the ability to claim such land as well as issues surrounding reclaiming any land that has been lost. It also discusses when and how a nation should be defended from attacks, along with factors about ending a war. There is also a short chapter on changes to appointing members to the supreme court. And finally, there is a chapter (that I thought would have been longer) about the tax system.

2.1 This Land Is My Land

The taking of land from others has happened for time immemorial. But, at what point does the previous owner of that land lose their title to it, and at what point do they lose the right to reclaim the land? I originally thought about this in relation to the pleas from Native American tribes asking for their ancestral land back. I had decided to work at this problem backwards since a solution would be impossible without knowing the surrounding issues of how the land was exchanged, how the land was typically transferred, and the time frame after the transfer occurred. But to dig into those issues, I decided that a base primer for land ownership and rights would be needed. This is not meant to be an all encompassing text on how land ownership needs to be altered within society. Instead, please view this more as an inherently long baseline to eventually solve an important issue.

Types of Transfers

There at five main ways for land to be transferred between parties:

- Force – The overt use of strength against another party to make them release the land ; War
- Coercion – The subtle use of strength against another party to make them

release the land ; Blackmail
- Trade - The open and willing exchange of land between parties for something in return ; Sale
- Gift - The open and willing exchange of land between parties for nothing in return ; Death
- Joining - The addition of another owner to the land ; Marriage

Each of these five ways to transfer are able to be done by both individuals or governments alike. A mobster can just as easily coerce a business owner to sell their property as a government is to coerce another country to give shift borders to stop a war or trade sanctions. Similarly, the use of force might be less likely to happen by individuals, but it will happen. Trade might be the most common form of transfer, but the fact that most coercive or forceful deals are made to look like trades can make things tricky. You can only know the deal wasn't a trade if the use of strength isn't hidden or was found out after the fact. While force and coercion are usually thought of as used by governments, the reverse can be thought of for gift and joining. The gift of land upon death to an individual is commonplace and happens all the time, while gift of land to the government does happen it is usually extremely rare. If the government does take possession of land, it is usually for a monetary sum (trade or coercion) or for a non-monetary allowance (to obtain a license or approval of a deal; or a trade) by the state. Usually, gifts received by the government happen when someone dies and either leaves it to the state or no living heirs can be found. Joining is another rare event for a government; while individuals or families combine resources quite frequently, most governments would refuse to join together even if their culture and customs are almost identical. However, the peaceful joining of two or more nations to form a single entity has precedent in history.

Rights of Ownership

The rights of the owner of the land is determined by the government or society the owner is a part of. If society at large has determined that no one is allowed to grow potatoes, then the act of growing potatoes is anathema to the society. Changes to the rules after the fact should be understood to allow certain stipulations to be grandfathered in, but flat out changing the rules surrounding the rights of landowners is within the rights of society. Similarly, if the land is owned by multiple people then the rules should be laid out in advance so that all parties can consent to any regulations. And if a change of rules is required, then sufficient notice and approval would be required to make the rules legitimate. The percentage of ownership should be considered equal in all parts unless expressly agreed to otherwise. This would mean that no one should be able to make unilateral decisions for the property without a majority approval from the other owner(s). To offset this issue, the government where this land resides might require an individual be named as a majority shareholder for all business with the property, but then the initial sale would be dependent on all parties expressly agreeing to one of them being named majority shareholder.

Rules of Exchange

What happens when one of the owners sells or modifies the property without majority approval? The easiest solution would be reaching majority approval after the fact, so the remaining members should first check to see if the deal as done, including distribution of funds, would have received a majority support of the shareholders. If approval of the existing deal is unable to be achieved, then attempting to alter the deal so as to make the majority approve is the next step. Alterations might have to include any seller and purchaser giving veto power to the new deal depending if additional money or property is to be used in the deal. For example, asking the purchaser to pay an additional $5,000 would need the express permission of the purchaser, with the purchaser able to veto the deal outright if they don't agree. Similarly, if the one that sold the property without majority approval is made to forgo their rightful share of payment from the sale and/or pay a monetary penalty would require their express permission. Veto power would also be given to anyone that is being made to forgo their rightful share of payment. If no agreement can be reached, then the property is returned to the original owners and payment is returned to the original payers. Legal action would then be a potential liability to the person that tried to sell the property without majority permission depending on the rules of the area.

The trade of land between nations can be fraught with difficulties due to the imbalance in power between individual owners and the power of the nation they reside in. Ideally, the exchange of land between nations would require the trade of land from the owner to the nation first. There is also the option to provide for ownership of the land in the new nation, but that comes with issues of new laws or regulations that were previously unknown or culturally different from the original county. But in reality, there is that chance that a nation that does not respect the people would potentially sell the land to another country without informing the current inhabitants or owners first and not reimburse them in any way. There will be some that use the adage of "might makes right", but a free country should respect the ownership of land within the country as if it was owned by a different country.

Rules that apply to any exchange of property is determined by the local government or society. Some areas of the world will have little laws on such exchanges and it will be done by trust and honor. Other societies will expect you to claim as much land as you are able to protect, if you are unable to protect the land you have claimed then others might force you off of it and take it for themselves. Local governments will decide the way they believe to be the easiest to determine that the transfer will not end in someone trying to "Claim" the land out from under someone.

A list of simple rules to make sure your transfer is unable to be claimed is as follows:

- Determine the current owner(s) of the property
- Determine who sold to the current owner(s) and if they were allowed to sell when they did
- Determine the local requirements to obtain the property
- Obtain a willing sale of the property
- Follow local customs for the sale
- Determine if there is a back-out clause
- Keep to your end of the deal from the perspective of the other party

The above rules are only applicable to a transfer by Trade, Gift, or Joining. An inherent use of power is implied for Force and Coercion meaning that a willing sale can never be done.

Bending of the Rules

If there is a cultural or societal rule for owning, selling, or using land that applies to your property, then is there a way around those rules. However, owners need to be very careful. Any rule that is in place will usually have an enforcement mechanism, so illegally building a shed on your property might not raise an alarm at first. But, when the house is put up for sale, a surveyor or inspector might realize the issue and cause the sale to not go through. As such, any permanent alteration to the property has the chance to be found out eventually and be traced back. Bending the rules for a permanent alteration is not worth the trouble. So what about non-permanent alterations? Anything that isn't able to be known beyond the property is realistically fair game. Imagine you have a heavily wooded property to the point where your nearest neighbor would never be able to see the cleared out area around your house.

Your daughter is about to turn 18, so you pitch a large 200 person tent in the clearing. Local laws might say you are required to get a permit to build such a large tent on your property. But, if no one from the property tells and no issues arise from improperly setting up the tent, then there is no realistic enforcement mechanism to worry about.

Issues can arise when it is two people bending the rules around a property they own together or where one is selling to the other. Full knowledge of breaking a custom or rule between the two interested parties is required, otherwise the ignorant party will have a chance to out the rule breaker. As an example of how to properly bend the rules, two brothers decide to purchase a property together. However, suppose one of the brothers is having marital issues that will lead to a divorce. Instead of putting the property in both of their names, they purchase the property in the other brother's name with the knowledge that both of them are responsible for the property even if the deed only says one of them is the owner. This is only possible with two people that trust each other implicitly and even then, great care should be taken by both brothers to codify the agreement before the purchase so that there are no misunderstandings. Both brothers hold risk. The brother with marital issues could refuse to pay his portion of the mortgage if the property doesn't work out the way they believe it would, and since he has no legal claim to the property there would be little to no repercussions. In a similar vein, the brother that has sole legal claim could refuse to split the profits with his brother. Any relationship between the brothers would be tainted by such action either way, but the possibility of being cheated is always present.

Intentional Ignorance

An issue can arise when one party keeps information secret from another party. There are three standard ways this happens, owner vs owner, owner vs regulators, seller vs buyer. The previous section dealt with the issues around owner vs regulators from the idea of limiting knowledge of what the regulators know on purpose. As well as explaining that permanent changes always have the chance to be found by regulators and then traced back to the owner that made the changes. Intentionally misleading or not informing any of these second parties is ill advised, but if you do choose to intentionally keep someone ignorant this section is meant to show the consequences.

Where a case is owner vs owner, the first distinction will be what kind of knowledge was withheld? Improper use of land that was already agreed was not supposed to be done means that the second owner should have a legal recourse unless no binding document was written up and signed. The legal recourse will change with local laws or customs as well as be determined on the type of use. If any permanent damage was done, or if the second owner wishes to suspend ownership of the property, then those factors count. If there is no signed document or proof of the agreement, then the second owner has less recourse unless the use goes against the area's standards and customs. If permanent damage was done or the second owner wishes to suspend his ownership of the property, then the second owner should have a case to seek damages or be bought out of their share of the property however they see fit. I would stipulate that the second owner should try to limit to anything that fits with local custom as they could then be taken to court for transgressing. Not informing the second owner of a known issue with the land is another problem that could happen in two ways, the first being before the sale knowing that the second owner wouldn't have purchased it if the issue was known beforehand. The other is if the issue was found during the ownership of the property and no attempt to inform the other owner was made. Little to no recourse is possible for the second issue, unless local laws and customs require strict information sharing between parties. Not informing the second owner may not make them happy with you but there is little they can do about it beyond what is always legally allowed for your area. An issue of not informing the second owner before purchase is much more serious. This should be seen as fraud and potentially have the ramification of jail time if serious enough. There will be different laws depending on the jurisdiction, but a court should try to allow compensation based on any lost money or potentially lost revenue. This is similar to the issue of selling a property without the other owner's consent, as detailed in a previous section.

Where the case is a matter of seller vs buyer, this requires another level of distinction that is inherent to this version of intentional ignorance and that is what level of issue is being kept from the buyer. Most people will expect someone to make sure they purchaser knows of any large scale damage to something on the property. For example, if you are selling a property with a shed that might look fine from the house or road but the entire back side of the shed and half of the roof is destroyed and is unsafe to be used, then not informing the buyer would almost always be in bad faith and allow for legal action to be taken. The issue comes when the issue is so small that it is either difficult to prove they knew an issue was present or that the issue was so small that it shouldn't decrease the price of the property in general. Such an issue might be that the shed from the previous example is in great shape except the rear door sticks in the summer due to bad hinges and wood swelling – that issue is minor and might be expected from general wear and tear of the property. Finding where that line is will be the issue for local laws and customs. Some areas might have a local custom that every door must work perfectly at all times and so selling a house with such a defect would be illegal. Other jurisdictions might expect such small issues to be expected, especially if the area has a lot of older houses with similar issues. Talking with a legal expert or realtor in your area is advisable. There is also the chance that you will be purchasing the home "As Is", and that should alert you to look closely at all parts of the house and to bring in a qualified inspector. Most properties or areas that sell with the idea of "As Is" have little to know recourse for the buyer unless the seller violated the law. And even then, the recourse might just be that the seller goes to jail and the buyer is stuck with the property. In a sense, the addition of "As Is" should be a benchmark for "buyer beware".

Who has a Claim?

Part 1 : Unclaimed Land

All property starts out as unowned, as a wild land that animals might roam freely. Someone might have claimed the land by saying, "I own all the land beyond that river," but have never set foot in any of the forests or built a fence around a field. All land starts out as unowned, and then an owner decides that they can subdue and hold onto the land in question. It might be hard to imagine a land that isn't claimed by anyone in the current era of satellites and airplanes, but what happens when the first person sets foot on Mars with the intent of putting up a fence and claiming the use of the land for their own purpose. Or what happens when a mining company finds an asteroid they would like to mine for the minerals? Are they not wishing to claim an area as their own?

Part 2 : The First Claimant

There are two ways that land can be claimed: a government or an individual decides the limits of the property to be owned. A government might claim more land than is currently needed but can at that time protect from invaders. This can take many forms, maybe a large river creates an easily defendable position and so doesn't need a completely solid border guard or individuals to homestead the entire length. Other such natural formations can cause this effect, mountain ranges, oceans, deserts, and jungles are some of the ways this can be achieved. A government could also force a large area to be claimed and then force any new settlers to homestead around the edge first leaving a large area in the middle to be unclaimed by any individual but allow the government to grow its land size easily enough. This large unclaimed land might be considered public property and anyone would be allowed to use the land as they see fit. Or it could be available for purchase by anyone who wishes to do so. The most common method for governments to claim land would be a blanket statement of, "We own everything that is that way," and will allow people to purchase or ask permission to "tame" the land as they see fit. You want 50 acres? Okay, pay me some taxes and you can mark out the fields or forest beyond Jim's house to your content, let me know where the boundaries are and I'll mark them down. The only obstacle a government has when claiming new land is making sure that other nations don't already own the land. If an individual owns land but is not affiliated with any other governments then they are acting as a government of one and has the choice of either joining your nation, being locked within their "national borders" and surrounded, war, or disbanding their claim to the land and leaving.

An individual can claim land for themselves or for a government to use as they see fit. An individual claiming land for themselves is little different from starting your own nation. Issues from starting your own nation can apply if the nation you used to be a part of takes issue with you creating your own country, but that is not an issue for this paper. If an individual claims land for their government there are unlimited ways that can be done because most of the details will be laws or customs from the government the land is claimed in the name of. Some nations will allow the claimant to take as much of the land as their own and develop the land as they see fit. Others might require a certain amount of acreage be given to the government and kept in good condition until an envoy can be sent to set up a satellite governing body. Lastly, some governments may require all claimed land to be given to the government; if the original claimant wishes to use the land they would be required to lease the land. All of these options and many more are possible dictates by the government the land is claimed for. No one can say which rules for an initial claim for a government is better, because the temperament and proclivities of each nation will change how the laws will be perceived and then acted upon.

Part 3 : Transfers

The types of transfers were described in a previous section and I will reiterate the information. But the important part to remember is that transfers can happen between individuals and governments alike. While a government selling to an individual might seem odd, it is possible. Here are the five types of transfers :

- Force – The overt use of strength against another party to make them release the land ; War
- Coercion – The subtle use of strength against another party to make them release the land ; Blackmail
- Trade – The open and willing exchange of land between parties for something in return ; Sale
- Gift – The open and willing exchange of land between parties for nothing in return ; Death
- Joining – The addition of another owner to the land ; Marriage

Part 4 : Post Transfer Regret

After the first claim to a land is made, the only way a new owner of the land can lay claim is by a transfer. Any peaceful transfer is made with willing participants, and as such any claim to the land would be null and void. Even if the original claimant regretted the transfer after the fact, there is no justification for going back on the deal. In fact it would inherently hurt the new owner to be deprived of the land after a peaceful transfer. As such, any original owner should be required to show proof that the transfer was in reality a forceful transfer before any legal system steps in to give the original claimant their claimed property. Again, local laws and customs will determine what information is required for such a claim to be recognized, so make sure that you provide evidence of coercion that is applicable to your laws. If no proof is forthcoming of a forced transfer then the owner and all of their heirs would lose the claim on the property in question. A person might regret a sale, but the sale would still stand, and there is always the option to purchase the property back.

Forceful Transfers are a different story. Regret after a forceful transfer is almost guaranteed, and as such would give a potential chance for legal action to reclaim the property. Proof is still required to be shown by the previous owner as explained in the above paragraph.

Regret is not always limited to the original owner of the property, a claim can be made by anyone sufficiently aggrieved by the forced transfer. But, there must be limits, so let's delve into who should have the "right" to be regretful. An original owner or any family of the original owner such as heirs or a direct descendant that would have potentially gained ownership of the property otherwise. The original owner's claim never fades with time. Family should be split into "potential owners" such as husbands, wives, children, or anyone that knows they were to inherit the property upon death, and anyone that is not in the first group should be considered as "aggrieved" for the sake of the original owner. Potential owners never lose their claim to a property along with the original claimant. Aggrieved persons lose their claim upon death and can't pass their claim onto anyone else. An aggrieved person is unable to pass the "love" of the individual onto someone else from death, as such since the only claim they had of the property was out of love for the original owner, the claim dies with the aggrieved person. Potential owners don't lose their claim upon death because their claim is due to a direct possible ownership of the property, so passing a claim to an heir is possible to any potential owner. Heirs are where things get tricky, so I will define an heir as anyone that can show they would have been gifted the property not from the original owner but from a "potential owner". Below is a diagram I have put together to help understand the ideas put forth in the rest of this part.

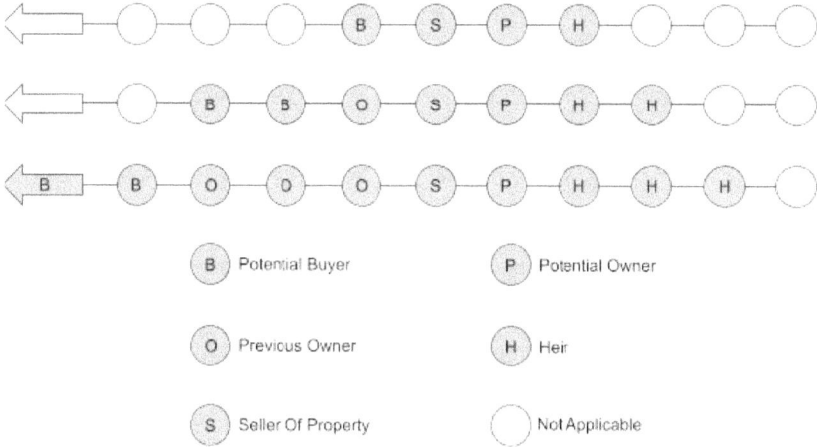

Any heir receives the right of regret, yet the issue arrives when deciding who is allowed to pass on the right to future generations. The main issue is how long the property has been in the family and if a clear line of succession has been defined. If the seller was the first or second owner in their family to own the property, then the first heir is unable to pass on the title of heir. If the seller was the third to fourth person to own the property then a second heir is allowed but can't designate another. If, the seller was the fifth person or more to own the property and a clear line of succession can be established for who the land would have been gifted to, then and only then can a third heir be established.

Part 5 : Group vs Individual

Any group that owns a property together that is forcefully transferred creates an issue. If the problem is due to some number of the owner(s) wanting to sell and one or more are holding out, then local laws and customs must decide the proper way to mitigate the issue. This was also discussed in the section called "Rules of Exchange". The main difference would also be that only a single heir would be allowed. Any property with a group claim is inherently a property with a more flexible ownership, as such, the ability for an individual to sell their shares of the property and potentially own majority right to the property out right expands with every additional owner the property has. Nothing much will change if all of the owners were against the transaction, only the potential person to make that will be required to pay reparations.

Part 6 : Country vs Country

Does the fact that a government has lost their land to another government change anything? Again, if the transfer was peaceful, then there is no claim to be had. If the transfer wasn't, then it should be viewed as a group claim. The only difference will be if the property can be considered as "Ancestral Land", to be defined as such the land has to have belonged to a country for over 125 years, then the right to have a second heir is allowed. I feel the need to explain that any citizen of the losing government born at the time of the transfer is seen as an original owner.

Losing a war that your government started is no different to a war that your government didn't start. Wars are messy, and losing one isn't desirable. But making the distinction of who started the war is usually left up to the winners, so giving the winners more of a reason to alter the facts of a conflict is ill advised.

Part 7 : Unhappy After the Fact

If a peaceful transfer of property happens and it is regretted later on to the point that you wish to reclaim the property then too bad. The property was properly transferred, you being butt hurt to the point of trying to hurt the current owner means you're in the wrong. Reflect on your actions and maybe stop being such a terrible person.

Reclamation

Once a claim has been made based off of a proven transfer involving force, it means that reclamation of the property is allowed. Any version where the claimant is an individual means they must go through the courts for that government, too many differences in laws or local customs will make it almost impossible to create a "one size fits all" guide. But, when the government is the one making the claim, there are 5 main ways of dealing with reclamation.

- Request – Asking the owners to transfer the property back due to the perceived issues with the original transfer
- Forceful Removal – Removal of the current owner(s) or tenants to a different area so that the transfer to the original owner can take place
- Temporary Detention – Removal of the current owner(s) and locking them away for a limited time as penance
- Permanent Detention – Removal of the current owner(s) and locking them away permanently so as penance and/or making sure it can happen again
- Death – Killing the current owner to make sure the transfer takes place

Talking to the current owners is going to be the most peaceful way to reclaim a property. A government agent explaining the situation and calmly asking for the property to be returned should be the first step in any reclamation procedure. This solves an issue for use of force when it isn't required and would potentially allow "cooler" heads to prevail. There might even be alternate solutions such as a monetary gift that would remove any regret associated with the original transfer.

Forceful removal is a good second choice if requesting the property back doesn't work. Removal of an individual from the land can become violent, so taking precaution to make sure any agents are safe during the removal is advisable. When dealing with another government this is considered an act of war, that is not to say it isn't a justified war or conflict but that the act of invading another country's land is an act of war that could have farther reaching implications than the land in dispute.

Temporary detention goes a little beyond the forceful removal. In the case of dealing with an individual, the government would be taking the property and locking them away for a limited time as a punishment or so that the transfer can go off without issues. If after being released the individual continues to harass or cause trouble for the reclaimer then the individual might need to be detained again. If another government has the property then temporary detention is an act of war by taking hostages. This would usually be done with the intent of ransom or leverage in asking for the land to be returned. These people would be considered POWs and shouldn't be mistreated while detained.

Permanent detention is exactly the same as temporary, but with no expected end to the detention. Local laws and customs would be the usual determination when permanent detention would be acceptable. Permanent detention of a POW means that the taking of prisoners was not meant to be used as a bargaining chip instead of going to war. Instead, the POWs were taken hostage with the intention of going to war in the end. It is a small difference that changes the entire breadth of the conflict.

Death. Such a final solution for reclamation should be seen as a last option. Even if the local laws allow for such an action, most should advocate against killing an individual that refuses to give back the property. However, if an act of war is committed then there is a good chance that deaths will occur during any conflicts. Needless deaths should be kept to a minimum, and the rules of just war should be obeyed at all times.

Now, how the initial exchange happened does change the acceptable level of force that is allowed to be used at the outset of reclaiming the property. A non-physically violent transfer will mean that all attempts should be made to request the property back. Any use of force, even just removal from the property could be seen as taking things too far. On the other side of the coin, an extremely violent and/or deadly exchange would mean you would be in your rights to retaliate in kind and be potentially deadly as well. There is a middle ground, where the original transfer was done forcefully but wouldn't have been considered a deadly situation, at that point use of force would be allowed as well as potential prosecution for any crimes committed. I feel the need to distinguish the difference between a criminal court and an international court for war crimes. It is not advisable, realistic, or in most cases legal to try to prosecute war criminals in a civilian court.

A civil war would be between two factions of a government that weren't separate before a conflict. So if a government splits into two factions, and the side that leaves while taking land without prior consent of the remaining side would be within their rights to try and reclaim the property. An occupation is when a government loses property and civilians to another government, allowing at some point that civilians from the old government can try to reclaim the lost territory for the old government from the inside.

Repetitive Conflicts

Now for what might be the most contentious part of this entire chapter, but the entire idea of this section is to stop blood feuds that last for hundreds of years and lead to dozens of wars fought over the same areas time and time again. After the first conflict has ended, and a second conflict between the same parties for either the same land or over a new territorial dispute the standard rules surrounding the end of a war are changed for the party that lost the first time. If the party that lost the first time wishes to enact extra stipulations such as removal of all civilians from the conquered area then this is a more reasonable position. If removal is hampered in any way, the violent removal to the point of killing should be looked down upon but not ruled out. Since multiple wars have been fought between the same groups, any left over civilian force could be an insurgency wishing to bide their time before another conflict. If a third or more conflicts has been started between both sides, any side that has lost two or more of these conflicts is entitled to complete violent ousting of any individual not from their own country when taking over land. This includes the killing of civilians that outright refuse to leave the area in an expedited manner. Every chance should be taken to reduce casualties from such actions, such as informing civilians that they have a set amount of time to leave and which direction they are able to go in, even patrolling the evacuation and providing food and water to civilians fleeing the area should be considered. But, if anyone refuses to leave or is taking an excessive amount of time to leave, then killing them should not be out of the question as they have decided to be considered an enemy combatant. Anyone with medical issues should be considered as POWs with the intent of returning them and a limited number of caretakers once they are stabilized to their home country or a neutral third party. At some point, repetitive conflicts will require the complete destruction of one side causing either the death of all citizens, annexation of citizens into their country, or the dispersal of citizens into other countries. This has other potential issues that have nothing to do with border disputes, some of which I will talk about in the next chapter.

2.2 Defense Of A Nation

One of the only things that a nation is almost universally required to do for its citizens is keep them safe. And usually that means at minimum, safe from other nations that wish them harm. So this chapter will look into the limits and constraints that a nation should be bound by when defending its people, and discuss what is acceptable or right to do after the conflict has ended.

Defensive vs. Offensive Use Of Force

While a pacifist mentality is preferable to one that encourages war between nations, a defensive use of force is the only moral stance that can be realistically held. If your nation is built upon pacifism, then you will eventually be pushed out of your land by those around you that don't subscribe to your ideals. Eventually your nation will be backed into a corner in which you are forced to either fight back, join the warmongering nation, or die. Death would be the ultimate end of pacifism on the world stage; this includes joining with the warmongering nation, as joining them means that your ideals and beliefs must die so that you can live with your conquerors. This means that the only way for your way of life to survive is to fight back. While your pacifism will be no more, the rest of your society will have the chance to survive. Now, if your society will devolve into either nothing or fight back against your enemies, then why not fight back against them when the aggression initially started?

What about being the nation that aggresses first? While the question of who started a conflict is arbitrary depending on the parties you ask, the initial use of force and why it was used is usually the deciding factor. Those factors are usually seen from the concept of "proportional response" which establishes the idea of using a similar use of force when force is used upon your nation. This can lead to passive wars, where "tit for tats" are exchanged for years with no clear winner because every action is in retaliation to the others retaliation. This can also lead to eventual increase in conflict as the response is gradually increased until an all out war is waged. As such, the first real use of force between nations is a barrier that no one should take lightly. In fact, I would go as far as saying that a non-defensive use of force is morally wrong and should never be used.

After a war has finished, the animosity for the other side will extend into any brokered peace. While the side that has "won" will usually be happy with the end of the conflict, those that "lose" will usually have a harder time with forgiving the winners. This can lead to a biding of time until a new force has been built up for a second war. Realistically, once the war has been concluded, all previous forms of aggression should be considered resolved. So any use of force towards a previous enemy without aggression first being used upon your side would be offensive instead of defensive. Such aggression should be seen as morally wrong not only because of the non-defensive use of force, but also because the use of force is charged with the animosity of the previous war and will more likely lead to a new war.

If an old enemy of a war has decided to retaliate and start a new conflict, then I would expect harsher penalties during and after the war has been concluded. This could take the form of certain limits that were placed on troops being lifted such as tactics to reduce civilian casualties or for what kind of peace can be brokered at the end of the conflict. In fact, ending the conflict will be even harder without total destruction of the opponents civilization due to the broken peace. This may seem harsh, but what would be worse is the creation of a "blood feud" situation where two groups fight for generations over the same issues and can never grow due to the feud. The extra pain and loss of life this would cause is immeasurable as the generation would continue, so harsher rules of battle as well as harsher treatment after the war is concluded is preferred. As an example, the expectation of fewer POWs after a war or of the outright killing of anyone found after a battle would become more reasonable as more and more wars are waged between the same people. Some of these issues are going to be unavoidable due to the outright animosity the soldiers will have for their opponents.

The above paragraphs are to articulate the moral and societal implications for offensive and defensive use of force. As a rule, this should not mean that offensive uses of force should be made illegal on its face. Starting a war should be frowned upon, but not illegal. Reason dictates that if we make the first act of violence illegal, then two things will happen. First, nations will become more secretive over their first uses of force to the point where false flag attacks should be not only expected, but encouraged so as to paint your enemy as "criminal" on the world stage. This is already used to sway popular opinion within a nation to fight back. We should not encourage extensive use of these tactics; those that would be the first to use force against another nation are most likely going to be the same people that would have no qualms about using deceptive tactics to paint their "enemies" as the aggressors. Second, we should not encourage for any reason a nation to try and change the history of why a war happened. The winners of a war have such power over the losers that if they wanted, they could force the losers to concede that the war was started via an unprovoked attack. So reducing the incentive for the winning side to retroactively change the history of the war is an imperative. To be frank, the issue is entirely a moral question; we should strive to make our nation as moral as possible in all things, let alone something as important as a war between nations. We grow morally as a people by understanding the issues and pains of the past and being determined to grow as a nation and do better. We are better, and we can be better.

When Is It Okay To Defend

The easy answer will always be once war has been declared. Open declaration of war is a time honored tradition that has made its way into the cultural fabric of the world, it's actually difficult to find a culture that doesn't have some sort of declaration to start a war. This probably stems from wars being between smaller nations and regions that had to deal with each other on a regular basis. If other nations found out that you started a war without notifying your enemy beforehand, then your ability to trade or move people through land would become rarer. While the attack on Pearl Harbor by the Japanese has been called a surprise attack, Japanese diplomats went through all of the proper procedures to declare war on the US before the attack began.

The more difficult answer to pin down is the "Act of War". As a term, an "Act of War" is used a lot in many different contexts to denote an extreme act that would spark the beginnings of a war, and usually meant for acts that would only be acceptable while in a war. Most don't realize that all acts of war besides open hostility and violence are at best situational to the parties involved. Most nations wouldn't go to war over the accidental killing of a national bird, it may create an international incident but wouldn't cause open conflict. On the other hand, what if the nation who accidentally killed the bird had actively tried to eradicate the bird in the past due to animosity between the nations. Such an incident could now rise to the level of an act of war depending on the past and current relations the nations have.

Such an issue arising over the death of a bird might seem unreasonable, but what about troops being placed on the border between two nations. The act of placing troops along the border is not hostile in and of itself, and that is the point. Nations with good relations can do military drills on each other's borders all the time, in fact they will sometimes do drills against each other to test out their readiness. Issues arise when the nations are not in good standing. Previous open conflicts between the nations will often make those in charge question the honesty of a newly deployed border force. Similarly, any nation that has been known to attack its neighbors in order to expand its territory will always be looked upon with suspicion, and so the placing of troops along the border could be seen as an offensive prelude to open conflict. So in such a situation, the use of a third party that both sides trust to patrol the border instead of their nation's troops could work to decrease tensions.

Not all acts of war require immediate open ground invasions to be sent; this is where escalation of force, de-escalation of force, or a proportional response comes into play. As a rule, the first time nations collide should be seen as a period to learn, so a de-escalation of force would be recommended to keep open conflict from starting. If de-escalation doesn't work, then a proportional response to the continued aggression becomes warranted. Each time a response is made, the nations should try for a peaceful agreement to past and present issues. At some point, a proportional response is not acceptable, tit-for-tat exchanges will eventually deteriorate relation between nations to the point of open hostility. If two nations have gotten to the point of open hostility, then proportional responses have been used too liberally. An escalation of force should be used when it becomes obvious that the two nations have started a never ending cycle of attacks based off of counter attacks that were themselves based off of other counter attacks. It is better to start a war and then finish it, than let side skirmishes that destroy infrastructure and livelihoods continue for years on end.

Who Can Defend

An obvious list of people would be a standing army or civilian militia, who have had some combat training and would be prepared for fighting in wartime. What about other civil combatants? Realistically, the people that are "allowed" to defend are those that wish to fight. Understanding of the horrors they are about to face are not necessary to fight for or defend a nation during wartime. Instead, anyone is allowed to be a combatant during wartime. Any non-combatant in a warzone is allowed to defend themselves or their nation. This is why all non-combatants should have been removed from a warzone prior to the start of battle, this does not mean that any civilians that are fleeing from a warzone are able to be slaughtered. Instead they should be either overlooked and allowed to escape or treated as POWs until the end of the battle, conflict, or war. Once a civilian tries to defend themselves with hostilities, they lose all protections of being a civilian and potentially lose the protections of being a POW. As such, any civilian that picks up arms against an invading army should understand that they might be killed; but what they might not realize is that they are also in trouble of being killed by their own side due to their own military not knowing which side they are on.

Limits During War

In this section, I will be breaking down the idea of what sort of limits are acceptable to be used during wartime and what breaking such rules will mean after the fact. This is by no means meant to be a treatise on the exact rules that must be followed during a war because the rules of war change as often as those who fight in wars.

No Rules

As an extreme, this is technically an option during wartime. Such a war is meant to be brutal, far reaching, and deadly to everyone. In fact, such a war should be seen as final to all combatants. If your side does not win, then your expectations should be set to total annihilation of yourself, civilization, and way of life. To continue down this line, it would also mean that the war will not end until all other civilizations that don't comport to this type of warfare are destroyed as well. Living next to a civilization that believes in and practices the idea of "There are no rules in war" is dangerous and should cause hostility between nations to fester. No true agreements can be made when one of the nations knows the lengths that the other would allow themselves to reach and is sickened by those possible actions.

Rules Of A Nation

Each nation has a set of rules that they follow outside of wartime. These laws are seen as the basis for a nation and what they believe to be either as moral or as "best practices". Some nations will alter what is allowed during a war to make it easier for their fighters to win, while other nations will make the rules and punishments more strict to keep a sense of community with the nation. But limiting your fighters to what is written into law makes it easier for those that fight to understand the rules and regulations of the war and how to act. Most people may not understand that there are laws that are directed solely at those that fight in wars and what they are or are not allowed to do during such times. But those that are trained to fight, will be trained on such rules and made to live them just as strictly as those rules for driving a car.

Rules You've Signed Onto

This is similar to the previous section, as these are rules that your nation has decided to follow, but the rules themselves were made from multiple nations working together to decide the limits of war. Such rules are usually either so broad to the point of making them useless, such a universal rule that most would have laws against it in the first place, or a direct rule that is intended to stop a practice that was used during a war. Signed-onto rules seem to be more about those rules that were deemed to be barbaric or immoral once they were actually used. As an example, the Geneva Convention forbids the use of chemical or biological weapons; the stated reasoning behind the ban is the lack of control such weapons have after they are used. A canister of gas can be released on the battlefield, and the wind changing direction can send the poisonous gas into a civilian area and kill thousands of unprepared civilians. This was added into the "rules of war" due to issues that were found to be possible during World War 1.

Your Enemies Rules

Your enemy in war doesn't have to sign onto the same rules that you fight by in war and you aren't required to fight by their rules. Issues occur when you have broken a rule that your enemy has for themselves but that you don't agree to, and then what is their recourse? You're already at war with them, what would the next step be? Realistically, the issues would be resolved after the war has been concluded. If you won, then the issue would usually be dropped. If you lose, then they may use your conduct in the war against you in peace negotiations or even ask to convene a court for war crimes. Each nation should determine if breaking your opponent's rules are worth whatever benefit you would gain from breaking them.

Signing Onto Your Enemies Rules

Before or during a war between two nations, they can confer with each other about what is or is not acceptable during the war. This will allow for the "rules of the game" to be set and agreed to by both parties. Rules can be seen as permanent or temporary; permanent means that your nation agrees that the rule is not just acceptable, but that it should also be a staple rule for any conflict in the future. Such rules become rarer the longer a nation continues to exist, mainly because the major issues of what rules in war are acceptable will be settled during the infancy of the nation's history or in between wars. Temporary rules can be specified by time frame or by a war partner. The "time frame" usually doesn't refer to a time period of years when the rule is "active," although it can, but it will usually mean that the rule will apply for a certain battle, theater of war, the war itself, or any war between where these nations are participants. Each of those temporary lengths can be an important signifier within the rules of engagement, as each of them would constitute a drastic change to instructing soldiers before deployment.

Breaking A Rule

If a rule is broken during wartime then the ramifications could be as small as disciplining a soldier or as large as being charged and killed for war crimes after the war. Realistically, there is no set way to deal with such issues during a war. A broken rule could lead to the other side breaking a rule which could lead to a tit-for-tat of rule breaking; this is why it is important to adhere to all rules of war and to view them all as equally important. With tensions flaring in the midst of war, it would not be impossible for some to decide that all the rules for war will cease to matter. If so, see the above section of "No Rules" for how that would turn out. It may be a good alternative to ask for a reconsideration of just that rule, if both sides agree that that rule doesn't apply anymore then that could solve the problem without devolving. This runs the issue of needing to have a reasonable talking relationship with your current enemy in a war.

As alluded to above, these issues could lead to a war crimes trial. While both the winning and losing side of the war can be subjected to trial, the winning side is usually less likely to be tried in a hostile court. If you have lost the war, you should expect to be tried under the rules of your enemy and not your own rules of engagement. It can be a defense that your nation doesn't believe in their rules of war, but it will be hard for a society to show mercy to those that committed what they see as a war crime against them. This does help to show that a neutral jury from a neutral nation should be used when a war crime trial takes place, it makes the decisions of the court more reasonable to those after the fact.

What To Do After War

After the war concludes, any issues between the still-recovering nations could easily result in a continuation of battle. Taking some time and making sure that all of the confusion doesn't cause larger problems is important. Issues of repatriation of the living and dead or what to do when the losing nation no longer exists can be lost in the shuffle after the war concludes.

Repatriation

Repatriation depends on the state of the person being repatriated and whether or not they are a POW. Civilians should be repatriated as quickly as possible, which would be helped by taking a census of those in custody so as to understand the scale of the issue. Any civilians should be treated well and with respect unless they fight back physically, this includes providing medical attention as well as more than adequate food and water rations. Both sides should expect to exchange their captured civilians for nothing except the release of their own civilians, and a non-combatant should not be seen as a bargaining chip for better terms.

On the POW side, repatriation can wait until the civilians have been returned, but a census of the captured should still be the first step. Treatment of POWs should be adequate for safety and health and realistically they should be treated better after the war than during. Torture and violence should always be discouraged, but if the prisoner fights against their guards then use of force should be expected. Only adequate amounts of food should be required for these prisoners; that does not mean that the prisoners should be left to slowly starve, but should not expect better food unless their captors have the resources to provide better types of food. Once the exchange of POWs is set to take place, remember that each prisoner should be exchanged for an equal quality of prisoner on the other side. Not all POWs are worth the same, but each one should be exchanged for another. If one side has a vastly greater number of POWs, then an issue arises of what they will be exchanged for. There should be a good faith effort on both sides to make a reasonable deal for the exchange of the remaining soldiers, so that neither side should be made to feel like they have lost. If the side that had the POWs feels like they lost, then they are discouraged from taking prisoners in the future. If the side that receives the POWs feels like they lost, then they are more likely to change tactics towards those that end in suicide vs capture.

After all of the POWs and civilians have been returned, the next issue is the dead. All dead should be returned to the side they originally belonged to. Respect for the corpses should be shown at all times and any funeral rites should be adhered to within reason. Any special requests should be accommodated, as long as the side that requested the accommodation pays for any associated costs. It should go without saying, but honor and respect should be shown to all of the dead, because it doesn't matter what their social, political, or military station had been.

Complete Annexation

If the "loser" of the war has lost to the point of completely losing all land and now no longer exists as a nation, then there are a few ways to go about treating citizens. The first option is to integrate them into your population, which comes with benefits and drawbacks that arise on a case by case basis. If the cultural heritage of the two nations are similar enough, then integration could be an easy solution. But as the original cultures diverge from each other, then the likelihood that integration would cause pockets of discontent to form within the nation increases.

Another option is to disperse the citizens into other countries as war refugees. Many might have fled to begin with; so asking if those nations that have taken in refugees can take more could remedy matters. Make sure that whatever nation they flee to is on good terms with you will also be important as you don't want to feed a nation that dislikes you a large population of people that have every reason to despise you.

While the historical baggage that comes with setting up a reserve or refugee camp within your border is largely negative, actually setting up a safe location for the losing civilians to go while decisions are made as to where they can go permanently can be a great option. This would allow for a military guard so that no one from your existing population can attack them due to animus over the war or for them to try and subvert your nation from the inside. In fact, this could allow for a slower form of integration into your society or other nations that are willing to take them but can't handle such a large influx of refugees. Individual families could show their ability to integrate into your society and as such, gain freedom from the camps. A less palatable, but also applicable option, would be the voluntary adoption of newborns from inside the camps to suitable families on the outside. This would cause more issues and moral questions to the point where it should probably be removed as an option, but a bad option that is still workable is better than no option at all. Total loss of freedom is personally abhorrent, so a recommendation that some semblance of freedom be left to those being detained can not be made vigorously enough.

The Less Than Savory

Trying to "weed" out the "bad ones" is just a losing proposition. How can you tell who are the ones that will try to subvert your government? The ones that get past you will be the ones you needed to catch in the first place. In reality, you can't weed them out. At best what you can do is to remove all possessions and then relocate them. If you find that someone is trying to hide a questionable possession, then they would be the closest thing you could call a weed. What you do with the weed is up to the severity of the issue at hand.

Extermination of all citizens of the losing country, civilians and military alike, should never be done. The very idea is repugnant, and should be thought of as such. Any nation that has tried to do this over the years has been recorded with infamy for their crimes and should be touted for the rest of time as barbaric. Eventually, a new nation will try this again and we must keep an eye out for the signs so that we can help those that flee and prepare for the eventual war that will take place. As no country that borders such a nation will ever feel safe, and nor should they.

Rebuilding A Nation

Before World War 2, common knowledge was that the losing side of a war was meant to pay the winning side for the costs of the war. This was meant to hurt the losers, to make it harder for them to recover and attack in the future. However, after World War I, the debt that Germany was saddled with is one of the major factors that caused World War II. So, after World War II ended, a new idea was tried out with both Germany and Japan. Instead of forcing them to saddle an absolutely absurd amount of debt and ruin their nation for at least a generation, the winners helped to rebuild the losing side. This has actually shown to reduce the conflicts and animosity between the warring parties. Citizens of the losing country are happy for the help and are all too ready to blame everything on the old losing government since, "they must have been wrong, these guys have helped us so much." Not every conflict must end in disaster and destruction, instead, a peace between nations and each side helping the other in rebuilding will do more good for future relations than the war ever would.

2.3 Supreme Court Appointments

Over the years I have found that a larger than normal emphasis has been placed upon the selection of Supreme Court positions. This does make sense due to the sheer amount of political power those seats hold. But, the political footballing that happens during campaign seasons for a seat that might not be available for 10 years is absurd. Furthermore, the advancement of medical technology over the years has made the old system of selecting a much rarer issue than it could be. So below I try and propose some changes to the system for appointing Supreme Court justices.

Lifetime Appointments

Lifetime appointments are wrong for any position within government. Maintaining a free government requires the free exchange of those in government; while that doesn't preclude a lengthy term of service, it does preclude a government bureaucrat from lording over citizens for an undisclosed period of time. What if one of the political parties became so powerful as to be able to appoint a 25 year old to the position of supreme court judge? They would be within their right to do so, as long as the Senate had enough votes. This could drastically change how a judge is picked, and how long a judge can stay on the bench.

Medical advances will eventually make the same issue but from the reverse. What's to be done when medical advances have made the average life expectancy of a person around 300 years of age? Does a supreme court judge that was appointed when they are 65 get to sit on the bench for over 200 years? Will there be riots because the newer generations will find fault with a person that grew up with the morals of 200 years prior? Is it really acceptable to have a position that only 9 people can be a part of, and yet allow them to be permanent fixtures for centuries?

This problem is worse if you take it from the position of not medical advancements, but from computer advancements. What happens if a human's brain is able to be downloaded into a computer? The computer would need to be transferred every right that a flesh and blood human would be granted. Otherwise, the forced slavery or the ability to spy on someone's thoughts, actions, or memories would be entirely allowed. So if a human's brain is transplanted into a computer and then appointed to the supreme court, does that mean they could take that seat indefinitely? A thousand years later, all supreme court seats will be filled by effectively immortal people with the moral philosophy of those from a millennia in the past.

How It Should Be

The first thing we must change is how they should be appointed to the position. A group of three should be nominated by the president at the beginning of each presidential term; they should be designated as primary, secondary, and tertiary so that a rank of seniority will be set before they are on the court. The three slots become available to the president after the first inauguration following a presidential election. If the slots have not been filled before a new president is sworn in, then the new president is allowed to nominate individuals to fill the seats. All available nominations are voided if not used by the day of the next presidential election, to prevent a President from letting their successor get 6 nominations. The three nominated judges are sent to the Senate for questions and then the group is voted on together as a pass or fail. There is no way to only pass just one of the nominated people and let the others return.

Each judge is allowed to serve for a term of 20 years, this should allow for them to judge for 5 presidential terms. If a subsequent president wishes to nominate you for another term that is fine. Serving for longer than 20 years was never the issue, the issue was that no one from the citizenry could object to the judge having a longer term.

Realistically the maximum number of judges is to be 15, adding up from 5 presidential races times three per race. The technical maximum number of judges is actually 18 due to the possibility that there could be an overlap in the 20 year term. On the other side, there should be a set minimum of 9. If the court falls below the minimum of 9 then a special round of nominations shall be set to take place immediately. The current President is to nominate a single person as the primary, the Majority Leader of the House of Representatives will nominate one person as the secondary, and the Minority Leader of the House of Representatives is to nominate a person as the tertiary. Just like a normal nomination process, the senate will vote on them as a group. If the court is still below the threshold of 9, then another round of nominations is to take place.

2.4 Changing The Tax System

I don't know about you, but I hate having to pay so much in taxes. This might be worse for me as a small business owner, because I get to see a multitude of other taxes and takings that the general public are oblivious to. I'm not a fan of how often and much the government takes from its citizens. So, this chapter is dedicated to listing certain ways the government receives money and how I believe things should be changed to make a fairer tax system overall.

Legal Takings

One of the more perverse incentives that is currently allowed in our society is when a government is allowed to fine someone a penalty and then use that penalty for their own purposes. Such a system is rife for abuse and would open the door for government agents to make unreasonable laws that care hefty fines for no other reason than to "legally" increase their yearly budget. Any fine or taking should never go directly to any government agency or contractors. Especially not the agency that has the authority to charge a citizen or enforce the taking. This also includes fines from a court going to the court or governmental body. Bad things tend to happen when the government has incentives to find people guilty so that they can receive more money.

Where Does The Money Go?

Not allowing the government to profit from a fine is one thing, but that doesn't mean they aren't allowed to fine their citizens. So where does the money go? It should be pooled and then given as a credit in equal shares to all citizens to pay off their taxes within the jurisdiction. This would mean that all federal fines and federal court penalties would apply to all federal taxes; while municipal fines or parking tickets would go to decrease the property tax for those that own property in the area that the fine was levied.

Distribution of the pooled money should be equally distributed among those that are eligible to receive the credit. The money is not to ever be distributed proportionally or equitably. A proportional distribution would be giving more of the credit to those that pay more in taxes, but that would cause the average person to barely receive any credit while the richest would receive the most. Equitable distributions are just as bad, for giving those that make less a bigger share of the distribution. Anything that affects the whole of society, which is why a fine is levied, affects us all equally; so we should all be entitled to an equal distribution of the pooled money. This means that anytime a large corporation is fined for doing something wrong and is forced to pay the government, they will actually be paying a portion of the taxes of every citizen they harmed by breaking the law. This doesn't negate the ability for a victim to sue for relief.

Any tax credits are to be stored in an account and saved until it can be used at a later date. Credits would be unable to expire, nor will they decrease in value over time. They are unable to be traded to someone else to stop someone from selling them at a loss for some quick money. But they are able to be transferred upon death along with the rest of their estate.

Taxes

I have never understood the reasoning behind a progressive tax system. In my opinion all tax rates should be the same across the board. This also means that there shouldn't be a different tax rate depending on the category of the income. All income is the same no matter if it's from a paycheck or in the form of capital gains. This doesn't mean that the idea of capital gains needs to be removed; deciding what is considered income can be important for a country to be competitive on the world stage. So to make it a level playing field, there should be no tax deductions for anyone unless it's a tax credit that has been given to all citizens that pay such taxes equally.

Since all tax credits are given equally, then the only way to reduce your own tax bill would be to reduce everyone's taxes. I would suggest the creation of a "poverty line," and then giving a tax credit to allow everyone to get to that line without having to pay taxes. This would allow those in poverty to use their money to the best of their advantage without needing to worry about taxes at the end of the year. It would also allow those that make less than the poverty line to build up a tax credit over time until they make enough money to use the extra credits they accrued over time. Since they don't expire and you can transfer them only upon death, a parent that never made much money in their life can bequeath their child a large amount of credits to use if they find themselves working a well paying job.

I have never understood the reason behind such a difficult to understand/use tax forms. In reality most people should only require their personal identifiers and 5 lines of information:

1. What did you earn?
2. Where did you earn it?
3. How much did you pay us?
4. How much of your credit would you like to use?

5. This is how much you own or are owed

This kind of information would be acceptable for most citizens and could be done on the back of a postcard. There wouldn't be any questions about depreciation calculations over time or deductible vs non-deductible expenses.

III

Money and Trade

A shockingly few number of people seem to understand the basics of an economy even though their lives depend on it doing well. So I delve into the issues of creating a monetary standard , along with some best practices in doing so. I look into solving what I see as major issues with a national budget. Next is a chapter pertaining to global trade, and what types of nations should be traded with. Lastly, I try to solve an issue surrounding the repayment of debt.

3.1 Currency Standards

Our nation's money used to be backed by gold. We were unable to spend or lend with impunity lest the bill was eventually cashed in. I see our change to fiat currency as deplorable and what will eventually lead to the end of our economy. I have tried to explain what a currency standard is and why it is important in this chapter. This will not be required to understand later chapters and will be overly simplified, but it will help explain what I see as our current economic state and why we should move towards a standardized currency again.

What Is A Currency Standard?

Historically, most nations have had or moved towards a currency that was backed up by standardized versions of commodities. For those that don't know, a commodity is usually an economic resource that can't be easily replicated or faked within the society. I would split them even further into perishable or non-perishable commodities. The difference tends to be that perishable commodities such as orange juice, coffee, and wheat have a shelf life that might be extended through technological advancements; while a non-perishable commodity such as metals, gems, or ivory are usually able to be left on a shelf indefinitely and used at anytime for its intended use. Choosing between these options will have drastic effects on the way a nation's economy will grow and evolve over time.

Perishable commodities can cause vast fluctuations in the price of goods an economy deals with. On a yearly time scale, any economy that deals in wheat as a standard will deal with immense inflation just after a major harvest and debilitating deflation during the winter months. Such fluctuations will stabilize due to knowledge that the issue always happens like clock work, but this is nothing until the entire economy is destroyed when a major drought hits the nation. Droughts in such an economy would mean deflation to the point of death or servitude for anyone that doesn't grow their own wheat.

Non-perishable commodities on the other hand allow for long term stabilization of pricing of most goods. This does mean that a balance has to be struck between the use of the commodity and using it for production of goods. This is why the use of precious metals for a standard is so popular. They can be easily divided without destroying the price, and using a metal to make products such as gold decorations still allows for the use of the gold in later trade. While certain parts of a nation's economy might experience inflation or deflation through the year similar to those nations using perishable commodities, the effects on the economy as a whole are usually reduced to the point where most citizens would be able to survive with some minimal planning.

Importance Of Having A Standard

Having a monetary standard for a nation's economy is important for ease of trade not only between citizens, but other towns and nations. Most fledgling economies start out with a barter system which is inherently difficult to quantify until the town creates a standard trade amount between different goods. This would usually show up as something similar to X loaves of bread is equal to Y cups of milk which is equal to Z pounds of meat; that essentially creates base values of goods without the use of money. Those amounts will still change over time depending on the supply and demands of the economy in question, but the micro-economy of a town will eventually equalize without any outside influence.

Large sums of wealth are then able to be made when traveling merchants are able to find the beneficial disparities between different micro-economies within the same nation. Town one might be close to a mountain rich in iron deposits but have a major lack of farmable land due to the rocky soil. Town two might have no iron at all but have vast acres of land with fertile soil and large trees for logging. So a single merchant would be able to go into town one and purchase a large amount of iron or ingots, transport them to town two, sell for a profit, purchase as much excess food and wood as possible, and then return to town one to sell the food. A healthy balance between these two towns would be created where eventually, enough food for both towns is made by town two and as much iron as both towns needs is mines from town one. Now, expand this to not just two or three towns. Expand this thought exercise to hundreds of towns and cities, all with their own amounts of exportable goods and fluctuating versions of what each good is worth for each town. This is why using a monetary system that is backed with a standard would allow easier trade between a larger area and allow for an easier discernment of pricing.

A non-perishable commodity that gets used as the standard only makes things easier for long term trades to take place. The ability to store gold coins away for when a drought happens, or when someone breaks a bone, and for an eventual retirement is only possible when the standard being used doesn't deteriorate over time. Similar currency standards that used things other than gold have been used as well, such as some Scottish villages that used nails. Droughts will cause the perishable commodities of an area to be worth less in an area without a drought; meaning even if you could use a perishable commodity to buy grain in a different town or city, the amount such a commodity could purchase would be less during such a drought. An issue of quality arises as well.

If every bushel of apples is looked at the same then why would anyone work to create a better quality of apple? Instead, wouldn't the profit motive be to make an apple tree that will create as many apples as possible without worrying about the taste? Lastly, the ability to split a non-perishable commodity like metal allows for easier fractional spending; having to slaughter an entire cow due to needing to purchase something worth half a cow makes things more difficult than splitting larger bars of gold in half.

Some Basics Of An Economy

The first part of this section will be used to break down the hypothetical micro-economy of a town of 20 people. Each person needs the equivalent of 10 units of money for daily survival. This means that each person must spend 3650 units to survive a full year, and this calculation allows for days off or for a person to spend a large amount of time on the production of one thing such as farming a field. If a person in the economy needs to spend 5 units to purchase enough materials to make the daily amount of 10 units in profit, then they would actually need a daily amount of 15 units. Each person within the town will need to make a similar calculation. But the idea is that each person would need 10 units plus the amount needed to purchase the materials to make those 10 units in profit. In this manner, a town of 20 can live off of a minimum yearly spending of 73,000 units. This doesn't mean the town needs there to be that many physical units in circulation, due to the units being traded on an almost daily basis.

In the hypothetical town from above, the money supply never needs to change once it's been put in place. The economy of the town will work because everyone is trading for all the other things they need. And since no money is lost or added to the system, there aren't any price fluctuations due to an expanding or receding economy. A similar effect has been shown to happen in communal living arrangements where all resources are pooled by the community. But as the population expands, the likelihood of leeches to the community increases. I think the technical limit of about 200 is reasonable with a strict rule set of everyone works, everyone eats, no slacking off. As you add more members to the community, the likelihood someone falls through the cracks increases exponentially.

Changes to the money supply of the town can have deleterious effects over time. If half of the town's monetary standard disappears overnight, then the cost of goods would halve immediately; while if half of the units of money are taken out of circulation then the real cost of goods would halve gradually over time until they all need 5 units a day to survive. On the flip side, a doubling of the monetary standard or money in circulation would also lead to prices doubling. This is only possible because there is no outside trade with other towns. As well, this shows how a perfect hypothetical economy doesn't need to worry what the monetary standard represents. The people of the town don't need to care if the unit of money is representative of an ounce of silver or 1,000 lbs of gold, they only care in respect of what that unit of money is able to purchase within the town. Trade between towns is when the monetary standard and how it correlates to the standard of other towns becomes important.

If trade between two towns is always unequal to the detriment of one of the towns, then the price of goods within the losing town will gradually increase due to demand and scarcity. That is, until no one in the losing town is able to purchase the goods from the other town anymore due to the total supply of cash in town not allowing for the purchases of goods from outside the town. At such a point, the town's internal economy would balance out to an equilibrium of minimum requirements for everyone to survive. This would mean no frivolous spending and only purchasing what is needed to survive such as food, water, and shelter. Even safety and clothes go out the window to a certain extent. This is why unequal trading can be detrimental if it continues in one direction for an extended period of time. Small but steady inequities can bring down major economies if there isn't something making up the inequality somewhere else. As an example, buying 100k of goods from another country and only selling then 50k worth of goods in return isn't functional long term; but what if those 100k in goods can be manufactured into 200k in goods to be sold to other countries? Your nation is now able to make a significant profit from the initial loss of capital.

The Printing Of Money

There are two main ways of "printing money." The first is just that, printing paper money without adding anything to the stockpile of resources that back the paper money. This can be extremely dangerous unless the entire economy knows such a thing is happening, and even then it can still be destructive to the economy if done in excess. In the short term, such a move can be beneficial but cause hyperinflation and removes all belief in the currency as a stable unit of measure. As such, printing money can only be a positive if the currency has no relative use outside your community. Even a limited amount of printing while not explicitly negative, I would not consider it a positive either. Printing any money without adding to the stockpile devalues all money in circulation and should be seen as a theft from anyone who holds that currency.

Option two is to add more of the commodity to the stockpile and then to print a complimentary amount of money to what was added. This will add more spending money into the system at large, as well as keep the value of all existing money at or around the same point it was previously. Adding money to the current supply like this actually might raise the effective price of the commodity in question, the reason being that any significant purchase of a commodity and then subsequent removal of that amount from an economy's normal flow of goods will leave a gap in the "supply and demand" graph of society. On a short term basis this might be true if the purchase was of a significant enough quantity; but on a longer term scale the price would fluctuate until it reaches a new balance within the economy, potentially bringing the price back to its original level. Another option would be that the people that needed the commodity, who instead of purchasing it from the sources they originally intended to, would cash out bills from a bank for an equal amount of the commodity from the stockpile. This could potentially lead to an almost immediate reduction of the stockpile by nearly the same amount it was increased by. This is usually limited by the usefulness of the resource in question. If a watchmaker can't find enough gold on the open market, but has the money, they can use the gold backed notes to withdraw gold from the bank's stockpile. This also shows that products that use the resource in question will retain some of the value as long as the production of goods doesn't destroy the resource.

3.2 Budgeting For A Nation

I have many issues with the way that America creates its budget. The politicians always want to spend more than they bring in until they aren't in office, then it's gross negligence that they are spending so much. We need a better way for the nation to budget.

The Three Year Plan

Collect, budget, Spend. Collect. Budget. Spend. It's really not that hard. It should be a three year process for determining how much money the Government can or should spend in a single year. The first year is when the Government should collect and tally all taxes and levies that the Government is allowed to use in its budget. This specifically means they shouldn't be allowed to print money for use in a budget. The second year is when the Government should use the tallied amount to create a budget. Such a budget should be either balanced, or leave some money left over as a surplus. In the final year, the money should be spent according to the budget passed by Congress. Not only that, but since this is done on a three year time scale, each of these steps should be being done simultaneously for different years. Why is this so difficult for the Government to implement?

Balanced Budget

A balanced budget should be a requirement for all budgets that don't meet a very strict level of scrutiny or high bar for need. Liability payments should be removed off the top as automatic payments that have previously been allocated and paid for. Such payments should be limited to payments on debt that was taken out during years when it was required to spend more than the nation had. If during the budgeting process, extra payments on the debt want to be allocated then such payments can be added in.

The limits for creating a balanced budget should be either during wartime or a supermajority approval from Congress. For a wartime scenario of increased spending, a few conditions are required. Firstly, Congress should be required to have passed a Declaration of War. Such a vote should be passed with at least 60% approval. The final wartime stipulation is that excess spending can't be approved solely on a "cold war" scenario, so that only a "hot war" can warrant excess spending. Supermajority approval doesn't match up with the historical meaning of a supermajority; instead I am referring to a budget being passed with the consent of 75% of both the House and Senate. Such consent should be calculated using total available seats and not just the seats currently being held or occupied. This also requires that if a budget is passed in multiple parts, then all of the parts must pass with the 75% minimum.

When A Budget Doesn't Pass

If a budget doesn't get passed during a year that doesn't mean that no money will be spent the next year. It also shouldn't mean that the budget stays the same, because that would incentivize doing nothing if a fight between new spending happens. So I have put together some calculations to show what I believe is the best alternative.

$$C_1 = \text{"baseline" or "last years budget"}$$
$$C_2 = \text{Money that was collected last year}$$
$$C_3 = \text{"baseline" minus 5\% ; } C_1 \times .95 = C_3$$

If $C_3 \leq C_2$ then Use C_3 as the new baseline, otherwise use C_2 for all further baseline calculations. This makes it so that every year that Congress doesn't pass a budget means that the minimum decrease in government spending will be 5% across the board; and in fact if the nation was unable to collect enough taxes, it could be much worse. Next is to find the percentage difference between the new and the old baselines and then decrease all line items on the budget by that percentage across the board. This new budget is considered as C_1 for the purposes of the next year's budget process if no budget is passed again. If a budget surplus occurs, then the remaining money is to be returned to the citizens in accordance with the chapter called "Changing The Tax System".

Underspending A Budget

What happens when an agency or fund doesn't spend the entire allotment they were budgeted? A fund might be meant to build up a reserve over time until an issue occurs that the fund was meant to alleviate. The law creating the fund must state how long the fund must hold onto the funds for; if not explicitly stated, then the time period will be considered as 1 year. An indefinite hold on the funds can be legal, it just has to be explicitly stated within the law. Such a fund would be similar to the Social Security Trust Fund; as the fund was set up to be used upon a person's "retirement", the ability for the fund to hold onto money is only limited by the ability for them to pay.

An agency on the other hand is only given a certain amount to spend and it must then spend that amount within that fiscal year. The possibility for the agency to not spend the entire amount is entirely plausible. If the amount is less than 1% of the allotted budget, then the agency will be allowed to save the entire amount for use during the next fiscal year. If instead the amount is greater than 1%, they will be required to return all but .5% to the nation's citizens. Any monetary return to citizens will follow those steps laid out in the chapter "Changing The Tax System".

Any fund that has been created and then given money can't be used for purposes other than what was stated in the law that created the fund. The only way to allow access to the funds would be to alter the available uses of the fund through passage of a new law. Anyone found to be using funds that were not meant to be used for the purpose they were used for in the end are to be charged and sent to jail. This is in actuality theft not just from the nation, but from all of the citizens of the nation.

3.3 Global Trade

Trading with other nations is important, so important that it can make or break our economy. We can also lead to us helping those that would do us harm. So why do we do it? Why do we help those that wish for nothing less than for our nation to stop existing? I propose a change of thought, I suggest we start asking why we should trade instead of why not.

Who Can Trade

In an ideal scenario, trade would be open to all who wanted it without limits set on what is being traded and in what quantity. That being said, a more realistic answer is anything but the most basic of trade goods can be traded with anyone that shares our values and traditions. As such, I have put together a list that I consider to be the most important values and traditions that our society has to offer.

- Anti cruel punishments - excessively cruel punishments should be outlawed
- Anti-slavery - must refuse to use slave labor in the production of goods
- Equal protections under the law - everyone is treated equally under that

law
- Freedom of movement - citizens should be able to travel freely within the nation
- Freedom of thought - thoughts should never be criminalized
- Gay rights - being gay should not be a crime
- Innocent until proven guilty - courts must prove your guilt before punishment
- Religious freedom - having the freedom to choose your religion without coercion
- Women's rights - women should have the same rights as men

These values and traditions are so important to our society that any nation that disagrees with them on a fundamental level should be seen as suspect and have reduced trading rights with our nation. This also means that we most likely don't share the values and traditions of their nation to the point where they should restrict the types of trading goods we should be able to purchase from them as well. As I see it, there should be a tiered system of trade that nations will be allowed to trade under depending on the number of values they share. Nine values means that 5 levels would be an acceptable number of levels if divided as shown in the table below.

Level #	# of shared Values
Level 1	8 or 9
Level 2	6 or 7
Level 3	4 or 5
Level 4	2 or 3
Level 5	0 or 1

As an important note, all of these trade levels are only applicable to nations we aren't actively hostile against. For example, it would make no sense for us to trade with a nation that we are at war with just because they technically fit as level 1. Especially since we would also have more trade restrictions against a nation that we weren't at war with, but was pegged as a level 4.

Types Of Goods

- Building Materials – Any material or equipment that is used in construction process; this would include but not limited to metal beams, concrete, lumber, and elevators

- Clothes (Basic) – Simple clothes that have no distinguishing characteristic to them and would be ideal for adding to or altering to make into a branded piece of clothing; plain white t-shirts or pants without a logo and doesn't include not include bags or non-essential clothing.

- Clothes (Designer) - Any clothing that has been manufactured to make the price more expensive on purpose; This includes all purses and bags as well as items from Versace, Gucci, and Prada.

- Consumer Goods - These are everyday items that someone might need or use to make their life easier but are not required to live; Staplers, cups, clipboards, and pens

- Food and Water - Any good that is to be eaten or drunk. That doesn't mean that it can't be used for other purposes, but that the alternative use must be highly unlikely, or using another product would be a better alternative

- Jewelry - Any watches, bracelets, or earrings; essentially, any item that has been made or embellished with expensive metal or jewels for the sole purpose of showing off wealth, or any item that is made to replicate such an item with inexpensive materials.

- Land/Property - Any physical territory within the nation ; Exception will be allowed for renting and a limited number of diplomatic properties.

- Medical Supplies (Advanced) - Larger or more expensive medical supplies than those that would be seen in an emergency trauma kit; MRI machines, X-Rays or Sonogram Machines are all good examples.

- Medical Supplies (Simple) - Any basic medical supply that might be found in an emergency response kit as well as any basic medical drugs that are unable to be used in the manufacture of potent narcotics. Examples are gauze, bandaids, splints, and pain relievers.

- Military Grade Equipment - Any tools or items that are used by the military due to their advanced nature as well as any item that can be classed as a weapon.

- Power/Electricity - Anything that will either provide or be used to provide electricity or mechanical power on a large scale, this also includes gasoline or diesel for cars and trucks

- Raw Resources - Any mineral that has been collected such as sulfur or salt, metals that have been mined in either their raw state or in an initial smelted state(bars or iron), lumber that hasn't been cut down to size for use in use in construction

- Technology(High Grade) - Advanced technological machines that would require specialized components that have a high level of computational power; Computers, newer TV's and certain Cars

· Technology(Low Grade) - Simple machines that require almost no to no computational power to complete its tasks; Old Cars, washing machines, refrigerators, and stand mixer

Limits On Trade

Types of Goods	Level 5	Level 4	Level 3	Level 2	Level 1
Clothes (Basic)	X	X	X	X	X
Food and Water	X	X	X	X	X
Medical Supplies (Simple)		X	X	X	X
Raw Resources		X	X	X	X
Consumer Goods			X	X	X
Clothes (Designer)			X	X	X
Jewelry			X	X	X
Technology(Low Grade)			X	X	X
Building Materials				X	X
Power/Electricity				X	X
Technology(High Grade)				X	X
Medical Supplies (Advanced)				X	X
Land/Property					X
Military Equipment					X

In general, free trade is to be lauded and encouraged. To encourage open exchange of goods between nations there should be limits on tariffs, bounties, quotas, and sanctions. The use of such methods to either increase or decrease the flow of goods between nations is in fact a hindrance on trade in the long run. Most of the time, such tactics are used by individuals that see trade between nations as a zero sum game that must be won or conquered. That is not to say that there won't always be winners and losers, but most trades between nations can be positive to both sides.

Changes To The Agreement

All of the above is to be considered applicable when both nations are playing on a level playing field. This should mean that a formal agreement between nations has been reached and agreed to. Such an agreement should initially fit into the rubric listed above, but while negotiations are ongoing, any alterations to the agreements should be entirely reactionary on our part. As such, if the other nation should be allowed to trade consumer goods but has decided that all trade of consumer goods should be restricted then there shouldn't be any changes. This is because the restricting of an entire sector of trade is not in itself a hostile act. The aim is for trade to eventually open up to all sectors of trade; but adding more restrictions will only cause other restrictions and sanctions to follow, so allowing the free trade of a limited set of goods is better than restricted trade of all goods. Any agreement is available to change if both parties agree to the changes, but our side should always advocate for the increase of trade without restrictions as well as the types of goods available for trade.

On the other hand, if the other nation wishes to add tariffs, bounties, or quotas into the trade agreement then retaliation is recommended. Such retaliation should be limited in scope as to try and perfectly hinder such sales in an equal amount that the initial tariff, bounty, or quota helped. So, if the nation in question added a bounty of $5 per gallon of gas, then our nation should institute a tariff of $5 per gallon of gas. This will return the price back to the initial price point and cause the offending nation to pay our nation a premium on every gallon of gas until they remove the bounty. In fact, I would suggest any law passed about trade in such a manner have a shut-off clause for when the other nation decides to revoke the bounty.

If a nation that is under sanctions from trading in certain goods but is able to receive them through a proxy nation then actions need to be taken. First, the proxy nation should be contacted to inform them of the issue to see if they will willingly refuse to do business with the nation to subvert the sanction. Next, if the proxy nation refuses to stop purchasing the goods for sale to the sanctioned nation then they should be added to the lists of sanctioned nations. But only for the types of goods being resold to the sanctioned nation. Such an issue is not only for sanctions, this is also applicable for any nation that tries to circumvent the issues of a tariff, bounty, or quota similar to the paragraph above.

Nations at war will usually restrict all trade. This makes sense from a strategic standpoint and from a point of basic logic. I will however not make such an action as hard and fast as to rule there will be absolutely no trade under any circumstances. To stop all trade means that the possibility to recover goodwill through trade is cut off, and if goodwill can help stop a conflict then it should have every right to try and stop the violence through peace. Now, the only level of trade that is allowed while at war would be set to level 5. And even that should be seen as rare and for purely humanitarian purposes.

3.4 Debt Repayment For The Non-physical

There is an issue in society where people are able to get into debt and then file for bankruptcy but have no physical assets that can be repossessed after they default. This will usually mean the individual's other possessions become viable for repossession until the required amount is paid. For example, going to higher education can be costly and leave the student in tremendous amounts of debt, so filing for bankruptcy when they own very little means they can't lose anything and their knowledge gained cannot be repossessed. So governments have had to make student loans unable to be defaulted on, and for good reason. But I think that the issue in question can be solved in a slightly different way so that it could be used for any debt in a similar situation and could even be a loan type that could be requested.

An example of a standard loan is an individual wanting to purchase a car for $25,000 and needing to get a loan to finance the car. If the loan is to be paid off over 36 months at an annual interest rate of 6% (compounded monthly). Then the monthly payments would come out to $760.55 a month for a total payment amount of $27,379.74 if paid on time every month. Suppose that the individual who financed the car didn't pay the loan amount for a few months. The interest would increase the amount to be paid for completion of the loan. Eventually, the loan company would repossess the car for non-payment. But if they were unable to repossess the car, the loan would continue to accrue interest. Now, compounding interest is the most financially dangerous part of this scenario. The interest is not calculated off of the original amount owed; instead, any interest that is not paid off within a month is added onto the amount the interest is calculated from. So the interest payments may start out small, and after a while they will become much larger than the original loan if not paid off properly as the growth of the interest payments is exponential.

My idea would be to create a set amount that a borrower must repay. This would potentially de-incentivise early repayment of a loan due to no financial benefit from early payments. But, a late payment would still affect someone's credit score and ability to take out a line of credit in the future. I would make it so that this new type of loan is unable to be forgiven through bankruptcy and can't trigger a forced sale of goods. Lenders would be almost guaranteed a certain return on investment (ROI) and could even receive the money faster without the drawback of the money decreasing total amount to be paid. In fact, the only way that this type of loan would be forgiven outright is in the case of death of the lendee. This would be due to the fact that the actual "goods" received from the loan are no longer able to be used.

Hopefully, this would reduce or completely remove the federal government's ability to give out student loans. It would incentivise banks to lend larger amounts to people going to school for higher paying degrees. I even see a benefit where they would rate each ROI by degree and school attended. This would mean that lenders would refuse to lend money to someone that wanted to go to school for a degree that wouldn't pay enough. This would also allow some students to get longer term loans for degrees that might not pay as much; or allow for lower payments upfront with a gradual increase in payment amounts as the individual gets settled into the job market. Eventually this should lead to lenders incentivising going into set degree paths early. In fact, changing majors could become more difficult as the bank might require approval of the change before new tuition could be lent. Banks might not allow a law student to switch majors into dance theory, or any other degree paths with a low enough ROI to pay back the current and future student loans.

A possible secondary effect of such a loan system would be tiered degree costs. Certain degrees would cost more to enter the program, while others would have a lower overall cost and be subsidized by the higher cost programs. This would incentivise colleges to push students into higher paying STEM fields and to disincentive underpaid degrees. It would also encourage colleges to help all students get placed into high paying jobs after graduation so that their ROI would incentivise lenders.

Originally this form of lending was thought of in conjunction with student loans and their inherent problems with standard loan processes. Certain ancillary benefits have become clear as I have worked through the problem. Any debt that has been incurred where repossession is impossible would be fairer to both parties if made to use this new form of debt. Judicial judgements could and should be made into this type if they are unable to be paid up front and all at once. Such judgments like child support, alimony, and parking tickets would benefit from not being able to discharge through bankruptcy but not being overly penalized monetarily for non-payment. This form of loan would still allow automatic deductions to be made from paychecks until payment has been made in full, but would not harshly penalize the lendee if the automatic payments tend to be relatively small.

IV

Social Issues

A nation is not entirely built upon laws. It is also built upon the morals and ideals of the people who flourish in society. In this section I begin with questions of immigration within a stable society. I talk about the positives and negatives of using spite as a positive outlet. Then a conversation of what it means to grow up, and how to plan for the future. Finally, what it means to be a parent for a child, as well as what I see as the responsibility of being a parent.

4.1 How Many Is Too Many?

I have noticed an issue within most Western societies where a nation will open its borders to immigrants every year without caring for the total number of immigrants already within the nation. This issue is also exacerbated by any illegal immigration that takes place that doesn't seem to hamper the number of total immigrants allowed to enter. Cultural homogeneity within a society is important for the survival of that society. Passing on the values and traditions of not only the original citizens but those immigrants that wish to share their own values and traditions is important for the growth of a society. When groups of immigrants are so numerous that they don't need to share in the experience of the nation they are living in, but can practice the traditions of their home nation without sharing those experiences with the native inhabitants, then an issue of dueling cultures is bound to occur.

My solution is to set a maximum percentage of immigrants that are allowed to reside within the nation. This allows for the actual number of allowable immigrants to be flexible depending on the population size of the citizenry. Most nations tend to allow set amounts through the immigration process each year with no thought to illegal immigration, asylum, or refugees. They also don't tend to reduce the limits once they are set, so any population decline in citizens is seen as superfluous information when dealing with immigration numbers. This can cause the citizenry to feel like they have lost their nation to an occupying force.

To combat these issues I would set the percentage of immigrants to 4%, which works out to a maximum level of immigrants of 1 in 25. As an example, given a population size of 350 million, that would mean 336 million are citizens and 14 million would be non-citizens. And once the cap on immigrants has been reached, the government would be required to wait for someone to leave if they wished to allow entry for another immigrant. These numbers are set to include legal immigrants, illegal immigrants, asylum seekers, and refugees. Non-native students and tourists that don't overstay their temporary visas are not counted in the 4%, but the family of the student are seen as an immigrant unless they apply for a temporary visa similar to any other tourist.

Until an immigrant has been proven to have left the country, they are still counted within the statistics of immigrants within the nation. As such, the main goal of this plan is for turnover. When a person decides to stay and help grow our nation without becoming a citizen, then the nation has decided that this person can provide enough benefits for the nation that it is worth them taking up an immigration slot permanently. If an immigrant instead leaves the nation, that allows a new person to immigrate in their place. Becoming a citizen should be the main goal of the entire process and every non-citizen should have a roadmap to becoming a citizen if they wish or be kicked out so that a new immigrant can try. Part of the benefits of becoming a citizen is that it doesn't just free up one immigration slot, because for every 24 immigrants that become naturalized, that frees up 25 slots. Technically a country has the ability to grow exponentially, but realistically that isn't possible as long as the roadmap to becoming a citizen is planned to actually help prospective citizens to integrate into society at large. This would also disincentivize allowing bulk immigration for large families all together. One alternative might be to allow a smaller section of the family to immigrate in the beginning, and then to allow for supplemental immigration over time as available slots allow. There could even be the option to allow a naturalized citizen to choose who is allowed to take their slot.

4.2 I Encourage Spite

Spite is the one negative emotion that I will always encourage someone to use.

I see spite as the intellectual use and display of anger. The inverse of intellectual use of anger would be the rash or emotional use of anger which is vengeance. Spite doesn't necessarily mean that your action is proportional or less than it would have been if you acted out of vengeance. Instead it just means that you have thoroughly thought about the situation and what actions you wish to take. Anger to me is neutral until you act out on that anger; I might be angry that someone cut me off when I drove into work this morning, but unless I act on that anger such an emotion does no damage. It is also important to distinguish spite from revenge; I see revenge as a deeper emotion that usually takes a person down a path of taking things too far. In fact, a lot of times revenge includes illegal acts while spite is usually associated with legal but unwanted acts.

If you choose to be spiteful, then take a page from the Count of Monte Cristo. The main character in the book didn't go on a killing spree as soon as he was out of jail. Instead he took time and crafted a plan to make sure that his enemies paid for their crimes in inventive and dastardly ways. You need not let your machinations stew for as long as he did, or make your plans so elaborate, and you should eliminate as much violence as possible. But, that is not to say that he didn't know what he was doing every step of the way.

The cathartic release that comes from knowingly annoying someone out of spite can be so relaxing for the one acting out of spite. This also creates a situation where the victim of spite could take such non-violent nudging as a chance to change their behavior. It's unlikely, but still possible. There is also a form of spite that is called malicious compliance, when you do what you have been asked to do knowing that it will fail so as to inconvenience the person that has asked. Such actions are a better form of spite because the person that has asked for the action to happen has no logical recourse when things go wrong.

Situations where anger, rage, and spite are present always have the chance to backfire. Mainly due to retaliation. You must always remember that just because you decided to take the "high road" and use spite, that doesn't mean the other person will, and there is that chance that they will lash out in anger when they find out what you have done. Be careful who you are spiteful too and why, because it is not a one size fits all solution.

Please remember, you are not special; I encourage everyone else to be spiteful with you just as much as I encourage you to be spiteful against them. This can lead to a "tit for tat", where each of you will be spiteful in turn as retaliation for each perceived slight. Eventually, both of you might learn a valuable lesson about the powers of friendship and how forgiveness is the real gift. In reality, both of you will probably hate each other and form an awkward truce when one of you accidently hinders someone else. Or one of you is arrested for taking things way too far and then spending the night in jail. So try and make sure that your actions aren't so bad that it causes retaliation. In fact, if you are left open to retaliation, then you should probably go back to the drawing board because you are acting out of vengeance not spite. Actions that someone doesn't have recourse to complain about is spite, as well as something that makes the other person look crazy for complaining about that is spite.

As an example, imagine you lived your entire life watching your father help out his brother financially. Every few months, he would give him some money because of one reason or another. But, behind your father's back his brother always demeans him and bad mouths your father to the rest of the family. Your father knows and does nothing because he believes that it is better to help family when you can. After your father dies, his brother comes to you for money. Spite would be to cut him out of your life entirely, no money, no help, no communication. And if he tries to turn the family against you for being selfish, you tell your side of the story. You explain that you stayed silent while your father was alive, but now that he is gone you refuse to view that man as part of the family. Nothing else. If others help him, that is fine, since they are allowed to do what they deem to be right. But you are allowed to be spiteful.

4.3 Becoming An Adult

What do you want out of life?

I would first recommend working backwards. Deciding what "You" as an individual expect out of the life you are going to live. What will the end of your life look like? Are you going to be living in a shack on a beach in Hawaii teaching people to surf and relax? Or would you like to own a ranch in Nebraska where you're able to raise a small herd of horses? What kind of partner, if any, do you want to be with when you're older? Male? Female? Will they work? Will you? What about kids? Their temperament? All of these things and more are important but not necessary to know ahead of time. Because, you must then think about what qualities the person you want to live with will be searching for. Same thing for what kind of job you will want or where you will decide to settle down.

But what if I'm wrong?

Expect that you will be wrong. Life is never, and has never been easy. Life will continuously send you curve balls, and your job is to overcome any issue life sends your way. Adjusting your plans over time to conform to your current situation will be important. What you want out of life when you're 10 years old will be different from when you're 20, 30, or 50. Even a vast or drastic change in plans is acceptable as long as the new goal you wish to attain will make you happy in the long run, and as well as making sure that the goal you've set is attainable. As a warning, don't change your plans just to change them and don't hurt your relationships on a whim. Destroying a marriage of 15 years because you want to do a one night stand is the wrong choice, and you should know better.

What if I'm different from other people?

Throwing away the wisdom of those who came before you is foolish. It's fine to break the mold by thinking differently and trying new things or being creative. But, most people lose sight of the fact that they live lives that are shockingly similar to their ancestors. Yes, we have made great advancements in technology, but most people in this world will work, marry, barely make enough money, have children, and finally die. Not always in that order, although death is final. But, most of them will be happy. If most people have found joy in raising a child, expect that you will also find great joy in doing the same. If certain sporting events bring untold joy to millions of people, then expect you could find an equal amount if you gave the sport a shot. Do not out of hand say that going to the opera is for rich snobs, since you might find that your life will shine brighter after the first time you listen to an operatic aria. There is always a reason why people enjoy the things that bring them joy, and it is not up to you to decide what is good for humanity.

Why should I learn that?

Taking the time required to learn or master a skill is never a waste of time unless you choose to never use that skill. One skill is never just useful in one situation, the same skill can be useful in any number of ways. For example, the steady hand of a master painter will be just as important for a welder or surgeon and vice versa. As well, several smaller skills can lead you towards combining together into a more important skill down the line. But, everyone should learn some basic skills for living.

- Learn an instrument - The coordination required to play an instrument will serve you well in life. The vast majority of people today are unable to play an instrument, so learning to play will allow you to stand out.

- Learn a language – A second language will help you understand people from other nations and how they live. You would be shocked by the things you can learn about a person just from the words they use on a daily basis.

- Learn to cook - You will need to eat everyday for your entire life. So why not know how to make the food taste better. It can also help you save money when times are difficult.

- Learn basic home repairs - Now, I mean you should know how to change a light switch and change a shower head. You should also know how to patch and paint a hole in drywall. But, it shocks me to know how few people know how to use basic tools like a screwdriver properly. Don't be like them, learn.

- Learn basic car maintenance - Learn how to do your cars basic maintenance and/or emergency care. Changing your oil and spark plugs might not sound that important, but knowing how to change a flat tire will always be important.

- Learn to wash clothes - The ability to do your own laundry will be an important task if you ever expect to live on your own and succeed in life. No employer will want to keep you long term if your clothes stink up the office or store.

- Learn to clean - Cleaning your house or apartment seems simple enough, but the hard part is keeping it clean. Learning to make sure the place you call home is tidy will do wonders for your mental health.

- Learn to balance a budget - Knowing how much money you have, how much you can spend, and having a financial plan that lasts for more than a week will make you better off than at least 60% of the population.

Don't you dare stop at these - Each of these are good things to learn and expand on. But you will never know when the knowledge to solve a rubik's cube will become important or fun. Learn about a skill, try it out, have fun, and if you don't wish to continue that's fine. You learned what you don't like to do. And that can be just as important.

But what can I do?

In conclusion, you should take control of your life. You're the only person that can. First you will want to make small changes to your lifestyle, with enough small changes, your entire personality will shift along with it. Just make sure that you are making changes towards the person you want to become. Only you can completely ruin your life, because you will always be able to claw your way back. Complete ruin means that you have stopped trying to make things better. You are in control of your own happiness and you are the only person that can make your life flourish.

4.4 Fiduciary Responsibility of a Child

I don't trust the government to do what is right by a single child. I trust some governments to do what is right by children as a whole; but once you're dealing with the absolutes of a single child that needs a variety of attention that can't be quantified, I am unable to believe in that government. Instead, we do and should give that responsibility to the parents of the child. We give them the responsibility to raise their children so that they will be productive members of society. As such, I deem that the parent actually has a fiduciary responsibility for their children. This includes the health, wellbeing, and upbringing that a child is to receive, and to prepare them for the world they are to inhabit.

Such a responsibility means that a parent should enjoy final say on any subject of their child's upbringing. With that responsibility comes duties: if a parent can be shown/proven to have done something that goes against the health or future well-being of the child, they are to be held responsible. This might mean being charged either civilly or criminally and then taken to court. Punishments could range from monetary damages, forced emancipation, and/or jail time depending on the severity of the charges.

As a starting point to determine a parent's violation of the responsibilities of a parent, we should ask whether parents have become a tangible physical danger to the child. Or, have they committed a crime against their child? I have decided to specify a physical danger due to the flexible definitions that constitute psychological harm. Self harm is not always the fault of the parent and their teaching methods; in fact, there is some evidence to show that the majority of children that try to commit suicide are driven by the issues they find at their government mandated school they are required by law to participate in. So unless the parent has been shown to have pressured the child into committing suicide, they are not to be held responsible. The chance that a decision will cause psychological damage to their child is not a criminal offense.

To me, this boils down to either active damage or passive damage on the part of the parent. Active damage should be seen as any damage that has been done on purpose or that the parent knew was likely to cause permanent harm. As an example, sexual assault is a physical harm to child it is perpetrated against and as such is right to be seen as criminal. On the flip side, passive damage is any damage that was not expected or thought to have occurred from their actions. From the above example, the psychological harm the child will have to deal with is passive. Each person's psychological trauma from such an experience will be different and will need to be solved in a different way. It is also difficult if not impossible to prove that the individual wanted to cause emotional or psychological harm through their actions. This doesn't mean that compensatory damages can't be sued for in civil court, just that it shouldn't bear any weight for a criminal conviction.

Mainly, this can be boiled down to including the legal concept of "Mens Rea", or the guilty mind. This term is usually used in law to describe the requirement for a person to have known and actively wanted the crime to be committed. Did the parent want to strike and hurt their child? Did the parent want to steal from the child? Many legal cases require the prosecution to prove that the defendant had the Mens Rea of the crime in question.

One way to prove the Mens Rea would be to prove a parent's apathy towards their child. Especially if they are able to prove the apathy for the child in the face of a known danger. I see this as exceedingly problematic due to the option of adoption that all parents are allowed to take advantage of. While apathy can be an element in a criminal case, there still needs to be physical harm to the child to prove the damages that were done. For example, pimping out your child is a physical harm. Sexual assault is a physical harm that is criminal, while the parents willingness and apathy for the wellbeing of the child being physically assaulted goes to prove the Mens Rea of the crime.

Much of the remaining chapter will be set to giving what I see as needed latitude for the raising of children. Raising children is not easy, there is no manual, and it is by no means one size fits all. So to expect all children to be productive members of society if raised the exact same way is ridiculous. By extension, we should not inherently blame the parents for every issue the child must deal with. As such, a sometimes excessive amount of latitude should be given to parents raising a child.

Teaching

   This might be one of the most broad and controversial sections for latitude, because unless the parent is purposely teaching their child to be a felon (not just misdemeanors, but felonies) then the society should have no say. I don't care if you believe they're being taught wrong ideas or in an odd manner. Continuing the beliefs and traditions of someone by teaching them to their children is always acceptable.

Discipline

   Most will accept that slapping the hand of a child is allowed when teaching them not to touch a hot stove top. Similarly, yelling at a child is allowed when you're angry at their behavior when they purposely pushed down a toddler at the playground. You might not like to see a parent that does such a thing, but that is not up to you to decide for such minor issues. Now the other extreme would be a mother punching their child in the gut or breaking one of their bones. These examples are not discipline, since they are malicious and can cause lasting damage. This can sometimes be hard to determine where the fine line is when you're a bystander looking in, especially because you don't know or understand the situation at hand. But you can always call the police so that Child Protection Services (CPS) can look into any allegations of abuse.

Medical

Similar to teaching, medical issues can be controversial. As a parent, you should have complete and absolute control over the medical decisions of your child. This includes but is not limited to what surgeries are done, medical interventions, or lack of medical care in general. One exception is if a parent is denying medical care to cause the death of the child; but parents can permit death to be a release from pain. Allowing a child to die because they were annoying to you is not allowed, but allowing them to die because of unrelievable pain can be allowed. The only other caveat for this section would be the parents ability to choose an entirely cosmetic and non-reversible medical decision against the child's wishes.

Privileges

A parent must by law give you food, clothing, shelter, and an education. Beyond that, everything else is a privilege that the parent is giving their child. Does the child want a cellphone? Does the child want a car when they turn 16? Do they want to go to concerts with their friends on the weekends? All of these are up to the parents' discretion.

Autonomy

This oddly enough has some overlap with privileges. As allowing a child to earn the privilege to be autonomous and to go out on their own can be an important milestone in a young person's life. So a parent must have the ability to choose when their child is allowed to have autonomy and how much of it to give. For example, will they be allowed to play by themselves in a playroom, or go out to the corner store and back by themselves?

One issue is to allow all of these concepts to be, in times, overly broad, because the morals of today are not the morals of tomorrow. And allowing a child to sue a parent civilly for actions taken in their youth that sound back in the morals of the day is a recipe for society to fail. Similarly, causing distress and even hatred is not inherently punishable criminally or civilly without a provable link between the actions taken and a mindset that didn't care for the wellbeing of the child.

V

Abuse of Power

I see the government as a tool for the betterment of its citizens. So anytime that a government abuses the power they hold, this shows that said government has their own interest over its citizens. First I look into the ways that police tend to abuse their authority. Next, I break down the changes that should be made to using emergency powers. I continue with the judiciary and what is needed to make the court system fairer. Lastly, I end with a plea for changing the system as a whole.

5.1 Police Misconduct

Over the years, there have been many things that officers of the law have been allowed to go without punishment. Many of the things below are considered acceptable or even as good police work. I plan to showcase the practices that I view as the most problematic in hopes that it will facilitate changes within the system of policing in the future.

Lying To The Public

Many police officers lie. In fact, many times, the lies are encouraged or forgiven to allow an officer to corner an individual into a confession of wrongdoing. This is wrong and should be stopped from happening whenever possible. When an officer lies to a member of the public and gets away with it we don't know if they were originally wrong about the law and didn't know, or if the officer is lying on purpose. What it does do is it will eventually erode the trust between the police and the citizens they are sworn to protect, because those citizens will eventually assume that all officers will lie for a conviction. And if an officer is used to lying, what is ethically stopping them from lying under oath?

Now I do believe that there are a limited set of circumstances in which an officer should be allowed to lie. If during an interrogation, limited deception should be allowed. But each of these lies should be documented and approved by a superior officer before entering the interrogation. This keeps an officer from making up things about evidence on the fly as well as to help limit any possible conflicts from evidence gained if the officer's deception was found to be beyond the allowable scope. In the end however, each lie or deception needs to be disclosed before any confession for it to be considered admissible or before the end of the interrogation. Such disclosure should be open and obvious to the point where there is no question that the individuals know that they were purposely deceived. Similar hurdles should be made when dealing with lies of omission; leaving out key details that could prove innocence is just as bad as fabricating evidence that proves guilt.

The second time that a lie is allowed is if a court order has given the officer permission. Such permission must be extremely limited to a specific investigation or day, as well as limiting what kinds of lies the officer is allowed to make in the course of the investigation. Such a lie might be that the officer is allowed to lie to any member of the public that wants to solicit them for sex during a sex sting. Allowing the officer to lie about the situation at hand would be important to the investigation and making sure that a judge signed off first would eliminate any confusion from the public. Now, any lies that were told during such an investigation would need to be documented, tallied, explained to the individual that was lied to before any charges can be administered. This might be lengthy if an officer is put under cover for an extended period of time, but that should be a major part of any arrest.

Officers should grow to expect that any lie that is told could get their entire case thrown out as "fruit of the poisoned tree". However, that is not to say that all lies are the same. If an officer lies due to a misunderstanding of the law or procedure then that incident is fine, and should be seen as a teachable moment. Such moments should include a warning, training by the officer or department, and/or possible desk duty. We want to encourage law enforcement to want to learn about the laws they enforce and be open to being wrong, so giving overly harsh punishments for non-malicious conduct is counter productive. Now, if the officer has been given repeated training on a single subject and still refuses to follow standard procedure and lies, then that officer has shown malicious intent. Any such blatant lies should end in either permanent desk duty or immediate firing from the department.

Dealing With Complaints

Complaints against an officer should be taken very seriously. They Should not be outright believed without evidence, but any complaint against an officer should be seen as a learning experience. That being said, the main issue I've seen surrounding officer complaints has to do with a refusal to accept them. A complaint should be allowed to be given verbally, written, as a video, with evidence, or without. If a citizen wants to give a complaint on the side of the road immediately after a traffic stop, then the commanding officer should make time to take the complaint immediately. In a similar fashion, a citizen should be able to drop a written complaint off at a police station one county over so that the officers can then deliver the complaint to the correct precinct.

No one that is filing a complaint should be made to identify themselves unless they feel safe enough to do so. They are not required to be a party to the incident in question. This does not mean that 5 complaints about the same incident will be treated as 5 different incidents, but that they will eventually be collected under 1 collective incident. Refusal to give a contact number or address is also acceptable. In essence, any officer that shows up to work to find a bare envelope with sheets of paper that contain a hand written complaint and no other information should be taken and logged as an official complaint. If an officer does try to force the citizen to provide their contact information, that should be seen as a potential abuse of authority. The citizen in question already has an issue with an officer of the law, forcing the citizen to identify themselves can cause them to worry about retaliation.

Not taking the complaint is just as bad. The only reason for not taking a complaint is if you as an officer are not qualified to take in a complaint. Even then, you should take the provided complaint (verbal, written, or otherwise), explain the issue, offer to take down contact information so that the person that is able to take the complaint can call for other information, and then give it to an officer that can receive it. Any officers taking a complaint (hopefully all of them) should be trained to understand the regulations and expectations of an officer that is taking a complaint. Any complaint that is received should be given a publicly searchable number that anyone can look into so they can tell what happened because of the complaint. Any unfounded refusal to take a complaint should be seen as corruption and should lead to immediate dismissal of the officer.

A public database should be available for anyone that is interested in complaints against an officer. Such databases are meant to be made and accessible in a way that stops any worry that officers will retaliate. As stated before, each case should have a case number that is easy to procure and that is easy to disseminate.

All of the above is leading to the issue of retaliation. Any hint of retaliation on an officer's part should be handled with extreme severity. Being outright fired without benefits if you were also in the complaint would be getting off lightly. Potential jail time for obstructing a complaint and retaliation against someone that has given a complaint about you should be on the table. If retaliation can be proven but you were trying to "help" a fellow officer, then you should also be fired. But anyone suspected of retaliation should be put on desk duty until an investigation can be completed. Retaliation can include but is not limited to unwanted following of the complainant, forcing to ID, or generally being petty.

Immunity From Prosecution

Officers should never be immune from prosecution. If anything, they should be held to a stricter standard than an average citizen. An officer should be allowed to raise an affirmative defense at trial showing that they were acting within the guidelines of their job. But a judge or prosecutor is not allowed to drop the charges on grounds of "qualified immunity". This is due to all officer conduct on the job being backed by the government they work for. And government power is only obeyed due to an inherent threat of violence, meaning any abuse of power should be seen as a violent act. The consequences of which should mean losing the ability to wield such power again and/or imprisonment depending on the severity of the act of violence. Abuse of power will otherwise lead to general distrust of government officials and the subsequent increase in crimes not being reported to the police.

Officers Playing Games

Some officers have the bad habit of skirting the rules or using their position and resources to tip the scales the way that they want instead of the way that the citizenry want. Some of these examples might seem trivial, but a small abuse at first can lead to the same abuse for nefarious reasons down the line.

An officer should be required to quote and explain any law that they are actively enforcing upon request. They should be allowed to look up the law in question for reference, but it would be recommended that an officer know the law they are enforcing before any encounter with the public. Part of this requirement would be to give a way to reference the law in question at a later date. Upon requesting the information again, an officer is not required to re-explain the entire law again unless a 15 minute time has lapsed since it was explained last.

This is because it will never be illegal to not understand the legal jargon that a law is written in, and any officer that tries to make not understanding the law a criminal act should be fired on the spot. Part of the job of an officer is to help make citizens aware of the rules they must follow on a daily basis. No officer is required to debate the nuances of a law, but they are recommended to listen to a citizen's argument to see if it is a valid argument. At worst, the officer should call their superior for help making sense of the argument. Otherwise they could always drop the charges.

Detaining a citizen should be seen as a very serious act when it comes to investigating a crime on site. So detaining them without an acceptable reason should be looked at very harshly. To stop the unwarranted detention of citizens, anytime an officer detains someone and then lets them go needs to be investigated. Why was the detention necessary? Did the officer overstep their limits? Was there a valid reason for suspecting a crime that was then resolved after the detention? And it better be a good reason, because there can be circumstances in which a detention will go from being warranted to unwarranted after some questioning. But an unwarranted detention will cause distrust in the community, such distrust can potentially be remedied with an apology and training for the officer. But, what happens when the officers in the area continue to detain individuals without cause? That leads to a permanent distrust of the police, especially distrust towards an officer who is willing to bend the rules on detention will most likely bend the rules to arrest someone as well.

Following or surveilling a citizen when no crime has been committed with the intent to identity can be done on a whim most days. This can be done to further a case against them or even just to identify the individual in question using a license plate or pulling them over for a bogus traffic stop. First amendment audits have been dealing with such retaliatory actions for years. Secret surveillance of a citizen should always be frowned upon and limited through court order. Any officer found to have broken this rule should lose their job immediately. Similarly if an officer has decided to identify an individual that doesn't wish for their identity to be known there should be no recourse for the officer. A threat of detention or arrest is an unwarranted use of force that is backed by the office they inhabit. As such, following someone to their car without being asked to escort them is considered harassment. Running their plate when they follow a car is an improper use of police resources. Pulling them over for a bogus traffic stop is intimidation as well as an unlawful use of authority. Realistically I think that these offenses should be cause for immediate dismissal. The best case scenario is that the officer was just wanting to get a name to fill out a form. Worst case is that the officer is trying to find out information so that they can retaliate against them at a later date. Now, realistically neither of those options are going to happen all that often, but the most likely answer of hoping to find a reason to arrest the individual is not exactly a good reason either. We should assume that the officer is actively trying to find something to punish the citizen with, which is not acceptable police work.

Process Is The Punishment

Sometimes, an officer will know that there is nothing they are able to do against someone that they believe has committed a crime, or that they just don't like. As such, they might decide to arrest them without cause and then drop all of the charges later. That harrassment makes the punishment the act of wasting time and money. I see this as vile. If the individual was driving, now their car has been impounded, they need to pay to get it back, and they have missed any appointments they were supposed to go to. This kind of punishment has almost no recourse and can ruin a person's life, and they might lose a job or custody of their child all because an officer wanted to punish them.

Charging anyone for a crime should not be taken lightly, so dropping charges should be seen as even more serious. If the charges were dropped within a week, the officer should be under investigation automatically as to why, they should be required to do training surrounding the arrest, suspension or desk duty if it keeps happening. If instead the charges were dropped after a week but before trial there should still be an investigation, training for the officer, suspension, and a monetary payout for the pain and suffering of the citizen. If charges are dropped after the trial has started, a press release vindicating the accused is required, automatic payment of money, possible suspension for both officer and lawyer, and a full investigation as to why it slipped through the cracks that long.

A solution would be for all departments to determine the distinctive points at which charges can be dropped and then determine an acceptable amount of times an officer's cases can be dropped. Keeping record of such incidents and then when the predetermined amount happens, a full review of all cases must be done. If it is determined that the officer in question used their powers to arrest unlawfully then they must pay remunerations, put on desk duty while undergoing training if it was the first time, or serve jail time if it continues. All monetary payments are to be made by the officer in question but is guaranteed by the municipality they are employed by. Officers are allowed to get insurance for such payments, and the municipality can require insurance by their officers, but at some point the insurance companies will refuse to give a bad cop a policy.

5.2 Emergency Powers

Emergencies are a certainty in life. Not all things allow for complex and detailed planning that will work to alleviate all issues that might arise. Sometimes a single leader is needed to stem the tide and make decisive actions against a threat. This is why the American President is the leader of the armed forces. America has a single leader if we enter into a war. For those instances where appropriate executive powers haven't been assigned, we should allow the use of emergency powers.

The issue with granting emergency powers is the fact that they are so easily misused or abused for the political or social goals of the one in charge. Many times there is no real emergency, but the ability to use extraordinary powers to attain a goal has blinded many world leaders to the obvious abuse of power. Usually there is no downside for the executive that calls an emergency and then invokes the powers granted to them. And many times there are little to no limits placed on the executive that chooses to invoke the emergency powers.

So let's change things.

First things first. The maximum length of any emergency should be 6 months. That doesn't mean that it starts out as 6 months and then you can extend the emergency after the fact. It means that 6 months after the emergency has been called, all emergency powers stop. This includes any rules or regulations that were put in place that haven't gone through the standard method of passing legislation or rules. There are no exceptions. If the federal government is unable to pass legislation within 6 months to solve the issues of the moment, then the emergency wasn't bad enough to warrant emergency powers in the first place.

Next, there is to be a person that is given control of the emergency. This can be anyone, but should hopefully be someone that is qualified to solve the types of issues that would come out from such an emergency. They must give up any other job or position they hold so that they can deal full time with the emergency at hand. All investments held by immediate family need to be put into a blind trust for the duration of the emergency plus 3 months. At the same time, all acquaintances will have their investments tracked for the same time period for any insider trading or money funneling. Protective details for the immediate family must be provided by the Secret Service for at least 5 years.

Potentially more important than the issue of control is over when the emergency can be considered to be over. So at the beginning of the emergency, there must be a clear and concise end point that is given for when the emergency would be considered to be over. If large explosions destroy large portions of a state's energy grid, then it would make sense to tie the powers to the clearing of the rubble, starting construction to restore power, and/or start the investigation into the cause of the explosions. The goals may not be possible to be completed within 6 months, but they are just a stop gap until legislative authority can be provided to someone that will permanently take charge. Similarly, if all of the conditions are met within a week, then that means the emergency powers should be given up before the time limit. This is not to say that at 3 months into the emergency the person in charge can't add more issues to solve. For example, it would make sense to start out the previous example with the goal of clearing the rubble and prep for construction. Then as the rubble is cleared, the goal of starting constructions should be added as well as helping cut red tape as much as possible. But as construction is able to continue without input from the top, making sure the investigation into the incident can be added onto the list of duties. That is not to say that all of those things should be handled by the same person during the emergency, but that it would not be unreasonable if the emergency demanded it.

Limitations should be placed upon the potential powers the person in charge can wield. Authority must be narrowly tailored to the issue at hand, so an emergency stemming from riots in the streets should have no need for the power to sell weapons to another nation. Similarly, a medical emergency doesn't give the power to change what is taught in schools. Now no one in charge of an emergency shall be able to call up or order military personnel to do anything unless the current Commander in Chief has given their permission on a limited basis. In fact, the only way that an emergency should be allowed to command the armed forces is if there is no Commander in Chief and line of succession has been eliminated, at which point, the emergency in question should be to keep the nation safe during a crisis while a new election for The President could take place. At some point, funding should be provided for the emergency. This could be a set amount that was previously put aside in a slush fund, maybe a set amount that any emergency would be allowed to spend, or the executive could be allowed to re-allocate money to pay for the emergency. I would suggest setting a max percentage of yearly government income so as to limit what could be spent initially with the understanding that the legislature could always allocate more funds if the emergency requires.

Finally, the discussion of what happens after the emergency has ended. Anyone that held emergency powers is to be immediately fired without question, this is to include anyone that was seen to have partial authority over the situation or that was given the ability to act in the stead of the official person in charge. This is not to say they are able to go back to their original job if they originally worked in the government. They should now be permanently barred from ever running for or holding a public office, they are unable to work for government at any level ever again. A lifetime ban should be instituted on lobbying in general. And their investments are required to always be placed in a blind trust.

5.3 Issues In The Judiciary

For all of the problems that I have seen from the legislative or executive branches of government, oddly enough the most politically motivated issues that I've seen have come from the one branch that was never meant to play politics, the judicial branch. Most often than not, most judges will use their own morality to influence decisions they write. And sadly, they will also use certain pretexts to refuse to acknowledge facts of a case or the positions of their opponents when they hold the high ground. Most of the time, this results in either bad case law or not allowing a case to go to trial. We should be wary of a judiciary that plays politics with the bench no matter the side, because those that set the precedent won't always be in power.

Most judicial leniency seems to be used in the form of sentencing mitigation. I am apathetic for those whose circumstances make us wish to be lenient on them, but our rule of law should be made to stand on its own. For we can never know the heart of a person that begs for forgiveness, does the crocodile tears of a sociopath not move us just as much as a grieving mother if we can't tell that one is the sociopath? We are fallible, so our laws must strive to be fair. As such, any pleas of emotion should be limited and bear little to no weight at trial. Should a prosecutor be allowed to show the jury the defendant smiling in their mugshot and say, "Does that look like a remorseful person?" No. Emotional blackmail shouldn't be allowed from either side. If the laws are too harsh, change them. If they are too lenient, change them. Do not allow an unelected judge to change the laws to fit the circumstance.

Why are prosecutors allowed to bully a defendant into admitting guilt? Prosecutors are well known to charge someone with more crimes than they can prove just to use as leverage to force a plea agreement. This leads to most people choosing to plea down instead of taking the chance with a large number of counts they may lose on at trial. To me, this runs afoul of "innocence until proven guilty." Fixing the issue will most likely involve changing the state's incentive structure. So, because we are presumed innocent if the state drops a charge, they are admitting they were wrong in the first place. As such they should be required to pay remunerations for any potential loss of money and time for having to deal with the court. Remunerations should be calculated on a per offense basis from calculating the expected hours an above average lawyer would spend on such an offense, times the hourly cost of an above average lawyer would charge. Now, I believe the time at which a prosecutor drops the charges is also important. So below is a chart that details what percentage of the total payment should be given depending on if the defendant was out on bail, how long the charges were pending and at what point the trial is at. So, they should search the chart for the options that apply and choose the one with the highest percentage of payout.

Automatically	Once charged	25%
Not Out On Bail	After 2 months	100%
	After 1 Year	50%
	After Preliminary Hearing	75%
	After Start of Trial	85%
Out On Bail	Trail has Ended, No Verdict	95%
After Trail	Trial has Ended, Not found Guilty	105%

As for bail, most courts today use bail as a way to punish the accused before they have proven them guilty. The original and stated use of bail was to guarantee the accused showed up for their court date and didn't flee the jurisdiction. Ideals of community safety and balancing the right of the accused to be innocent until proven guilty was difficult to manage when the constitution was being written. Technological advancements have made the requirement for pretrial detention for most crimes ridiculous. Tracking software that can be used with leg collars and cell phones can make sure that no matter where the defendant goes, they can be tracked and made sure they don't flee the jurisdiction before trial. Adding on the availability for at-home drug tests means that most potential felons could be allowed to spend their days before conviction in their own home and allow them to continue working. Such a system is currently thought of as "bail reform," but the current systems put in place for such reforms have a major flaw. Low level re-offending, where a defendant can be released dozens of times on low level offenses, can occur due to the strict nature of the rules surrounding bail reform. So the idea of viewing the third low level offense as a felony that would require a higher level of accountability in the bail process could help keep the community safe until a trial can take place.

Many laws are too vague or are written in a manner that makes it almost impossible for the average citizen to understand the meaning of the laws they are subject to. In my mind, if any lengthy review of a law is necessary by the court to determine the legitimacy of the law in question, then it is too vague. This builds on the legal concept of lenity, but I posit that more restrictions should be put in place for when a judge rules on a motion dealing with lenity. Any legal arguments the state makes dealing with lenity should be limited in time and scope as to limit the ability for the state to go into the weeds of legal theory and how it applies to the law in question. This should also include a page limit for all briefs on the matter. Honestly, this type of motion should be made purposely difficult on the state so that any expansions of a law are made by the legislature and not by twisting the legal definitions of words within the law itself.

One of the more confusing aspects of the legal system is the issue of standing. Most believe that anyone can sue anyone else they want, and while that is true, the ability for the lawsuit to move forward without a motion to dismiss is another question. Standing is a term that references the ability for someone to sue. Three requirements must be reached for a person to have standing. They must have suffered an "injury in fact," said injury must be linked to the case brought before the court, and a favorable decision will redress the injury. None of those three aspects should matter and should mean that the idea of standing needs to be altered or thrown out entirely. Requirement of an injury in fact means that anyone that is trying to stop a law from going into effect would be unable to bring a suit to stop the law as there hasn't been an injury yet. In the legal field this is called "ripeness," and one should always be allowed to bring forward a case that stops an illegal action from happening before it happens. The injury being linked to the case at least makes sense if the first part was acceptable, but the requirement of the injury again leaves out the ability for someone to preemptively thwart an illegal law. Lastly, the issue of redressing the injury, this would exclude all plaintiffs that had their rights violated temporarily but have since "regained" their rights. Are we to say that the issue has truly been resolved? Could the issue or similar issue happen again? Was fair compensation given to the victim? As an example, this correlates with the previous section on dropping charges when the charges weren't warranted in the first place. Because the suit was dropped, many judges will consider the issue as "moot" since the redress of injury would be the dropping of charges and that has already occurred.

Everyone should have standing under that law, if for no other reason than for the ability to clarify a law in question. There could also be a situation in which a person wishes to make a factual representation in a court record and wishes to bring forward evidence. Such a record would be useful for defamation trials or for allegations of professional misconduct. The only reason a person's standing should be revoked is if a law explicitly bars a category of people from bringing a claim in a narrowly tailored manner. Such as a provision barring non-doctors from bringing a case that requires knowledge only a doctor would know or be privy to.

Not allowing a case that the plaintiff took too long to bring in front of a court (this is the legal doctrine of latches) should be extremely limited. In fact, unless the law in question has a specific section that denotes a statute of limitations there should be no legal way to limit such a case. And, any statute of limitations for civil crimes should start from the time the plaintiff learns of the issue at hand. But, if the solution being asked for is a change in the law, then latches never apply.

If you are in a court of law, the laws being read and then decided on are read using one of three different types of scrutiny. Strict scrutiny is when the bill is read verbatim and has to match the word and meaning of the bill in question. Most people would believe that this is the only type of scrutiny that the law should use, and they would be right. No law should be vague enough or interpreted to mean something that it was never meant to have meant. If the law is flawed, then the legislature should be forced to change the law.

Otherwise, judicial activists are able to change case law as they see fit and alter how the rest of the nation is run without a proper vote. Intermediate scrutiny is less rigorous and is usually used by courts during discrimination cases due to the inherently uncertain aspects in proving a crime has been committed. I am not against a set standard for certain types of crimes that determine guilt, but any "test" should be detailed within the law so as to make sure that every judge is accurate across the board. And the only way a court should be allowed to disregard the test is if they find it to be unlawful, and would then subsequently use strict scrutiny in its place. Rational basis is the final level of scrutiny, and in practice this is the easiest bar to pass since it only requires a legitimate state interest. Unfortunately "a legitimate state interest" basically comes down to whether or not the state doesn't like you for any reason. What would be legitimate? How could you prove it isn't legitimate? Using rational basis for any reason is antithetical to the founding beliefs of our nation and should be removed entirely from the courts.

I feel as if it should be said that a lot of these issues with the court would need to be amended simultaneously. Some of the changes by themselves could cause larger issues if not altered with another change at the same time.

5.4 A Plea For Change

This chapter will be different from all of the other ones. As I compiled the information and topics that I wished to discuss in length similar to all of the others, I realized one thing. That most of the issues I wanted to discuss had already been dealt with in other sections. That most of the issues in some way would just be references or rehashing of already discussed topics. So, I decided to change things up. This chapter still goes over the topics that we have discussed previously, but instead of a clinical view, I give a heartfelt emotional plea.

The Plea

The federal government has overstepped its prerogative by a wide margin and needs to be reigned in. They serve at the will of the people, and the fact that they are using that power to hurt the nation as a whole is despicable and needs to be remedied. If not, there will come a time in which the blood of this nation will be shed. I hope to never see that day come, and to be honest, the stopping of that future is easy enough. We many disenfranchised are not requiring the upheaval and change of the entire government at the same time. Most will be happy to encourage small but steady changes over the years, even if it comes with some setbacks. We believe in the steady flow of ideas. We believe in constant debate. We demand our grievances to be heard. And woe is the person that does not hear our warnings of collapse, because we are not the ones you should worry about. You should worry about the ones that believe there is no turning back.

All governments have proven without a shadow of a doubt that they are unable to handle the ability to keep their own secrets. The ability to post "Top Secret" on the top of a document and make sure that it stays hidden at the bottom of a deep dark hole is too great. It's shocking how many times there have been great troves of documents that get declassified and more often than not the information that was deemed secret poses no risk at all. And while that's bad, the issue is worse when you realize that the agents of the government fought tooth and nail to keep them secret even a day longer. And for what? The other end of the coin are the documents that will never be released, the amount of documents that no one even knows exist and that prove things that only conspiracy theorists dream of. I believe there should be certain limited amounts of information related to military secrets that are kept as secret for a limited time, or that wartime secrets will stay secret for the duration of the war they are a part of. But, each set of document types should have to fight to stay secret. There should be no more bulk secrets that only become available after 50 years, with the government swearing up and down that they had no hand in it, only to find out that the government did plan the whole thing and made some theorists look crazy. Such an action is a travesty and those responsible should be ashamed.

No government should have a say in what anyone has to say about anything. I worry for the day that a government agent will ask my son to alter the words on his post a bit so that it doesn't offend the sensibilities of his neighbor. Will he comply? Why not? It's only one little post. What's the harm in changing a few words? E-ve-ry-thing...We are only ourselves when we are allowed to think our own thoughts and express them to others. To change our words is to change our very being. To stop a line of questioning is to stop what makes us great as a species, what makes us great as a nation, what makes us great as ourselves. Do not stay silent, do not speak what they tell you to say. Fight. Fight for the right to be wrong. Fight for the right to offend. Fight for the right to be free.

It is so infuriating that our laws are so large and dense that no one is able to actually read them. Why can't an English teacher decide that their students will read the newest bill on the floor of the House of Representatives over the week and then write up a 3 page response to the bill as an assignment? Making the legislative process impactful in our everyday lives is important. I would actually consider listening to a podcast that all it did was read out the different bills that have been voted into law if they weren't 300 page monsters that not even the people voting for the bill could read in time. Hell, at least if they were required to read the bill in the chamber in its entirety before they could vote on it then these 300 page bills would take weeks to pass instead of hours. And why are Congressmen allowed to vote on a bill they have never read? That should be illegal. They should be required to sign a paper saying that they have read the entire bill before they are allowed to vote on the bill. And they should sign the paper under penalty of perjury.

What might actually make me madder than the length of the laws that are passed is all of the laws that are never repealed but are also never enforced. If an officer refuses to enforce a law, that is corruption. The issue of an outdated law is not one of the police that are required to enforce it, it's an issue for the legislature that refuses to repeal the outdated law. There are so many laws that we must obey on a daily basis, and they should all be seen as chains around our necks. "Show me the man and I will find you the crime," was not just a promise, it was a warning for those that value freedom from tyrannical government action. Everyone breaks the law at some point, if all it takes is for the government to look hard enough to find the link of the chain that someone has broken. Don't allow them more links than necessary. Make sure that older legislation dies off – if it's important enough they will vote to reinstate the law. But make them fight for it. Make it difficult for the legislature to take away your freedoms every time they want to.

Who allowed bills to be omnibuses? They should be ashamed of the idea that has helped ruin the soul of this nation. Nowadays, a bill that is supposed to be about forest conservation efforts in national parks will have line items about ice cream vendors in major metropolitan cities, budget allotments for DARPA spending, and tax breaks for electric cars. What in the world does any of that have to do with forest conservation? It doesn't, and we all know that it doesn't. But we also know that the bill wouldn't pass without greasing the palms of a few Congressmen for their votes. And that's the problem. If the bill can't pass on its own, then good. It's not popular enough to pass. Try again later when you have popular support. Too many bills nowadays are filled with so much fluff that the fluff seems to outnumber the actual legislation. And we allow it to happen because some of that fluff goes to our state, or has helped us pass the legislation that we wanted. It's all untenable and needs to stop, and the sooner the public realizes that and does something about it the better.

Governments should never be in control of the flow of money in a society. Every time a government tries to help out by making money flow to "the correct places", they end up screwing up more than just a few sectors. Even if it starts out amazing and everyone is happy, the lack of incentive to change will eventually make the service they provide insufficient for the world as it has changed. In a normal economy, the business that refuses to change will be out competed by those that advance. This is how economies are able to thrive. In fact, recent history has proven on more than one occasion that governments stepping out of the way allowed the economy to grow versus when they decided to step back in and the economy lost all of the growth it was able to secure. We must force the government to at most choose a currency standard for the nation, keep a stockpile of the standard, back deposits from theft, and require truth in banking standards. It's not hard, and we the citizens should have the ability to trust that our economy is not run on the whims of random men in suits that are just guessing what should be done. The intricacy of the national and world economy is staggering, so believing that any group of individuals could do a better job than an open market is ludicrous. If you believe otherwise than I have a bridge I want to sell you.

Global trade makes no sense as it is currently structured. Why are we allowed to trade the same types of goods with both China and Europe? Why? Seriously, it makes no sense. China is known to have deplorable social and economic conditions, and they openly admit to having different values from us. That is fine if that is how they run their nation, but we shouldn't be allowing the trades of goods on a level similar to the nations of Europe. Europe at least shares if not all, the vast majority of our cultural, traditional, and legal values. The types of trades we are allowed to make with other nations should be dependent on the types of values we share, because allowing their nation to thrive off of our values will only encourage more of their values in the future. Especially when we allow the sale of our most valuable and nonrenewable resource, land. Why can a Chinese national purchase land in the US? We should have strict limits on the ability for foreign nationals to purchase land, but we just allow anyone with a dollar to buy up the land from under us.

The fact that our elected leaders are not only unable to pass a balanced budget by themselves, but also rewarded for not balancing the budget, is just staggering. I loathe the fact that this was never thought of and made into a constitutional amendment. There are reasons that I can think of as to why it was never done, but they are all bad. We should all spend within our means, and government spending within its means should be no different. But, once again, the government has proven beyond a shadow of a doubt that it can't handle freedom, we must treat the government as you would a 5 year old with a dish of candy: absolute vigilance and a firm rule of how much they are allowed to have. Now, I understand that emergencies happen and that spending might need to increase accordingly. But constant emergencies that never seem to end is just understanding that there is a new way of life. We must understand and thrive within that life. But part of thriving is to live within our means. At some point, we must take the candy bowl away and only give them what they are allowed to have.

Immigration to our nation can't be unlimited. If we offer free programs to anyone that is in the US, then we can't let everyone in. I wouldn't mind nearly as much (but I still wouldn't be happy) if the government didn't require hospitals to provide ER care to anyone that shows up regardless if they can pay. The government is making its citizens pay for medical procedures of those that are here illegally. They also give large amounts of welfare and social services to anyone that needs it, including illegal immigrants. Now, if you're here legally, that's not a problem. I'm always happy to see someone that is meant to be here receiving a helping hand when they are on rough times. But the issue is that since we allow so much illegal immigration, there is no way to tell who is actually meant to be here or not. This causes distrust and sometimes will lead to violence. Instead, our laws should set a percentage of the population that is allowed to be immigrants. That limit should allow the majority of society to be citizens so that we can show those who immigrated here why our nation is so great. Show them our values and traditions, and allow us to see and experience theirs. We can celebrate what makes us different more easily if we are able to integrate as a society, and allowing mass immigration on the scale we have let it to occur makes everything more difficult.

Honestly, a lot of this can be brought back to whether or not we should trust the government to monitor themselves for wrong doing. And in the stupidest ways imaginable, they have proven incapable of any basic oversight. Most of the time, any government official will be happy to defer to authority automatically. So any checks or balance that has been put in place will eventually lead to those in charge of checking not doing their job and instead allowing the government free reign to do as they please. To be honest, I don't know how you should solve this issue. Because even if you were to make it mandatory that all government officials are to release all documents and information they have come in contact with on a weekly basis for open access by the public, they would still find a way to bury any real malfeasance on an encrypted form that no one knows to check. There would be some random bureaucrat that was never elected but has spent 30 years working a desk and decides that he knows best for the public and acts against the elected President. I would actually put money on it, because I would probably collect within a year.

Secret agencies seem to control too much of our society. There are too many times that a high ranking official from a government agency has gone before congress and lied about their involvement in undercover operations against American citizens. And then, 30 years of denials and smears calling people conspiracy theorists later, it turns out that they knew that whole time that they caused the problem, or killed the guy, or funded the group. And every time, they say, "Oh, no. They used to do that back in the day. But, we stopped all that. Believe us, we're on your side." No they aren't. They are liars, backstabbers, and thieves. Every organization that I know of has a large group of workers that believe in the values our nation is based upon. But without fail, every position at the top is almost invariably filled by those that had to play dirty to get there. Some will deserve loyalty and praise. But most deserve scorn and derision. The problem is that you can't tell the difference when they're behind the veil of secrets. So we must purge out society of all agencies that would do us harm from the shadows, stop them from taking aim without our knowledge, because they will invariably aim the crosshairs upon us.

Every action a government takes is backed by the threat of violence. If it wasn't, then there would be no reason for the government to be involved in the first place. No law is a request. No law is a plea. Each law is a demand at the end of a barrel of a gun. Such threats should be limited in scope and applicability so that the citizens retain the majority of their rights. Unfortunately, that is almost never the case. We become accustomed to laws and the "new normal" too quickly. We become complacent and are willing to accept new laws that paste themselves over the existing ones. Now we hardly feel the weight of the dozens of elephants that ride on our backs. We are not free, we have been made to serve, we have been made to be quiet. And all of these things have been done at the point of a gun.

Epilogue

I hope to find you contemplative at the end of this book. I have strived to explain many of the grand issues that I believe plague our society and make us stagnate. I am not the most knowledgeable of men, and I don't think myself so great that I can solve such great issues without help. So I have made this book in part, to put these ideas into the minds of those that will determine the future. I hope that this work of ideas and beliefs will be understood and passed on to those that will take in account the beliefs of a man that loves this country and all of the people that come together to do great things.

We are bound by laws that no one can know
and that all must live up to

We are a land of rules
and we must make sure they never falter

We are ruled by money
but we don't have to be

We are a nation divided by more than just borders
but we must find the bridge to help those we can

We are run by the corrupt
and it is up to us to weed them out

We must hope
for without hope
we are lost

www.ingramcontent.com/pod-product-compliance
Lightning Source LLC
LaVergne TN
LVHW052028080426
835513LV00018B/2217